D0097927

JOYCE'S CITIES

J O Y
C I T

C E’ S

I E S

Archaeologies of the Soul

Jackson I. Cope

The Johns Hopkins University Press

Baltimore and London

Printed in the United States of America

The Johns Hopkins University Press, Baltimore, Maryland 21218
The Johns Hopkins Press Ltd., London

Library of Congress Cataloging in Publication Data

Cope, Jackson I
Joyce's cities.

Includes bibliographical references and index.
1. Joyce, James, 1882-1941—Criticism and interpretation.
2. Joyce, James, 1882-1941—Settings.
3. Cities and towns in literature.
I. Title.
PR6019.09Z5273 823'.912 80-8856
ISBN 0-8018-2543-1

For Paula,

whose love fired a phoenix
in a desert.

"It's Phoenix, dear.
And the flame is, hear!"

CONTENTS

PREFACE

What follows is an imaginary coursing of stages in James Joyce's imagination. That is hubristic enough without admitting that it seems to epitomize the way those ancients we postmodernists call modern imagined the future through the past, imaged permanency as that continuing resurrection of sameness which forces or frees history to overlap itself into shapes we call myth.

Dickens's little waif had led her grandfather through a city as ghastly as Dante's, and one we continue to recognize as modern. Then, or at some other imaginative moment in the later nineteenth century, we learned that where we lived was how we live. Learned it again. Augustine's Rome would become a model of historical morality for Dante's Florence, just as that city would devolve into an imaginative touchstone for Burckhardt only twenty years before Joyce was born. But throughout his lifetime (throughout what we properly recognize as the modern) shovelers were uncovering the artifacts, the evidences of old times in older cities. It was the way one still lived, displaced in space and imagination, so that archaeology gave the inevitable a frisson of reality. Mutant as its details might seem, the modern was a self-conscious moment at which metaphor had transmogrified back to beginnings, having become not only mythologies, but a felt mystery. Both myth and mysticism were Joyce's natural heritage. I attempt to demonstrate this and to adumbrate its consequences for his fiction.

ACKNOWLEDGMENTS

An earlier version of chapter one and parts of chapters four and five appeared in *Genre* and *James Joyce Quarterly*, respectively. I wish to thank the editors of those journals for permission to reprint these essays.

Professors Peter Bailey and Hugh Kenner have read the whole with that keen scepticism and kind encouragement that earns any author's most honest gratitude.

My debt to Professor Diane Fortuna's perspective cannot be acknowledged properly in the few footnotes below because I only gradually realized its impact as I tried to teach myself how to read James Joyce. She was the first of those students whose stimulus and enthusiasm have made this book long continue to seem worth writing. The most enduring companion among them has been Peter Bailey. We have been teaching each other for a decade now.

A NOTE ON EDITIONS

D *Dubliners.* Edited by Robert Scholes. New York: Penguin Books, 1976.

E *Exiles.* Edited by Padraic Colum. New York: Viking Press, 1951.

SH *Stephen Hero.* Edited by Theodore Spencer, John J. Slocum, and Herbert Cahoon. New York: New Directions, 1955.

PA *A Portrait of the Artist as a Young Man: Text, Criticism, And Notes.* Edited by Chester G. Anderson. New York: Penguin Books, 1977.

U *Ulysses.* New York: Random House, 1934.

FW *Finnegans Wake.* New York: Viking Press, 1947.

L *Letters of James Joyce.* Edited by Stuart Gilbert and Richard Ellmann. 3 vols. New York: Viking Press, 1966.

I

THE WASTE LAND

> Each historic civilization . . . begins with a living urban core, the polis, and ends in a common graveyard of dust and bones, a Necropolis, or city of the dead; fire-scorched ruins, shattered buildings, empty workshops, heaps of meaningless refuse. . . .
>
> Lewis Mumford, *The City in History*

> Cityful passing away, other cityful coming, passing away too: other coming on, passing on. Houses, lines of houses, streets, miles of pavements, piled-up bricks, stones. . . . Piled up in cities, worn away age after age. Pyramids in sand. Built on bread and onions. Slaves Chinese wall. Babylon. Big stones left. Round towers. Rest rubble, sprawling suburbs, jerrybuilt. . . .
>
> *Ulysses*

Joyce was the father of modern literature. He remade the short story in *Dubliners* and redimensioned the novel repeatedly in three successive experimental masterpieces. To demonstrate the nature of these powerful renewals will be the burden of this book, as it must be the primary aim of all critical assessments of Joyce. But to see properly the nature of Joyce's modernist revolution, one must not lose sight of Joyce the Victorian. He planted his fictions firmly in the novelistic tradition of his great predecessors by unquestioningly assuming that the matrix of the psyche's conflicting alienation and need was the family. This conception of the primal social unit, so foreign to the couples, the strangers, the dangling men of later fiction, provides the narrative thread of all Joyce's fiction from "The Sisters" through *Exiles* and the Dedalian histories in myth into the incestuous labyrinths of *Finnegans Wake.* Further, Joyce followed his great predecessors in embedding both the individual and the family in the yet larger social (or antisocial) network of the city, a metaphor for the disparateness and lonely sterility of modern life from Dickens through Hawkes.[1] There were imaginations among the Victorians powerful enough to see this all too realistic vision of the modern city also as a mythic vision, to see London as T. S. Eliot would see it in *The Waste Land,* a return to and continuity with Dante's city of dead souls: "A crowd flowed over London Bridge, so many, I had not thought death had undone so many." The young James Joyce learned from them how to turn some brilliant glimpses of the turn-of-the-century Dublin scene into the first collection of stories that was ordered as a metaphor of the modern psyche. He meant it in a structural as well as a social sense when he wrote to Curran in 1904: "I call the series *Dubliners* to betray the soul of that hemiplegia or paralysis which many consider a city."[2]

I

It seems everywhere, this vision of the wasted and despairing city, if we map our landscape within the boundaries of those seventy years which lead up to *The Waste Land.* Reviewing Alexander Smith's youthful poems, Arthur Hugh Clough suggests that they seem to satisfy the need for a new poetry giving beauty to "the black streams that welter out of factories, the dreary lengths of urban and suburban dustiness." Indeed, "there are moods when one is prone to believe that, in these days, no longer by 'clear spring or shady grove' . . . are the true and lawful haunts of the poetic powers; but . . . if anywhere, in the blank and desolate streets, and upon the solitary bridges of the midnight city, where Guilt is . . . and pale Hope, that looks like Despair."[3] The Scotch anti-Pre-Raphaelite Robert Buchanan's *The City of Dream,* "an epic poem," leads a wandering pilgrim from his own dark city in search of the City of God, but in Book XI he enters "The Valley of Dead Gods," a waste land of dead phantoms from Apollo to Christ, and so abandons his search to enter the ephemeral "City of Man" (Book XIV), where Christ is another name for phantom Death. Gissing's

London slums were even more explicitly Dantesque: "This life you are now leading is that of the damned; this place to which you are confined is Hell! There is no escape for you . . . at the end there is waiting for you, one and all, a death in abandonment and despair. This is Hell—Hell—Hell!"[4]

Later Virginia Woolf, that great misunderstander of Gissing, is as awkward as he and as aware as he of Dante in surveying the spiritual landscape of London: "But this city we travel . . . Leave there to perish your hope . . . Bare are the pillars; auspicious to none . . . 'Good night, good night. You go this way?' 'Alas. I go that.'"[5] Or Beatrice Webb in her autobiography (*My Apprenticeship,* published in 1926) could say of London day laborers: "They do not migrate out of the district, but are constantly changing their lodgings: 'They are like the circle of the suicides in Dante's Inferno; they go around and around within a certain area.'"[6]

The vision and the voice of Dante are ubiquitously echoed by Joyce's generation and that which preceded it. Dante, the sensitive democrat and mystic of two generations of Rossettis, of Longfellow, of Mazzini, was never more popular than at the turn of the century,[7] but he was no longer the early Victorians' Dante. He was, rather, the visionary of the Florentine *Inferno,* a more modern role than that foisted upon him by Vincenzo Botta and other political modernizers.[8] Let us take as exemplary a text notable for its explicitness and intensity and for the fact that it contains several elements that are similar to elements in the work of Joyce, who may never have read it: James Thomson's *The City of Dreadful Night.*

In 1857 Thomson had written "Doom of a City," an allegory that might seem a first study for the later poem. The first section of this "fantasia" is "The Voyage," in which the narrator creeps from his home while "the mighty City in vast silence slept," creeps out "accurst," with "hopeless doubt which gnaws the brain." He is determined in this despair

> To leave my kind and dare the desert sea;
>   To drift alone and far,

> Dubious of any port or isle to gain,
> Ignorant of chart and star.[9]

The speaker's boat is beset by a storm, by a sea monster that dissolves into the metaphor of his own loosening of the tentacles of despair, and then he lands upon the shores of a vast city. His own, in simile, had been like a deserted, "buried City's maze of stone" ("Voyage," II). The city at which he arrives is the literal lapidation of that phrase:

> What found I in the City, then, which turned
> My deep and solemn hope to wild despair?
> What mystery of horror lay inurned
> Within the royal City great and fair?
> What found I? Dead stone sentries stony-eyed,
> . . . .
>
> Stone statues all throughout the streets and squares,
> Grouped as in social converse or alone;
> Dim stony merchants holding forth rich wares
> To catch the choice of purchasers of stone;
> . . . .
>
> The whole vast sea of life about me lay,
> The passionate, heaving restless, sounding life,
> With all its tides and billows, foam and spray,
> Arrested in full tumult of its strife
> Frozen into a nightmare's ghastly death,
> Struck silent from its laughter and its moan;
> The vigorous heart and brain and blood and breath
> Stark, strangled, coffined in eternal stone.
>
> ("The City," VII)

As the narrator passes through the streets of this dead-living city, a reader of Joyce is reminded of the inevitability of the lapidose metaphor for isolation in the midst of men: Seymour Bushe's eulogy on Michelangelo's Moses, which J. J. O'Malloy recalls verbatim ("that stony effigy in frozen music, horned and terrible, of the human form divine" [*U*, 138]), appears in that section of *Ulysses* which concludes with the sterile clack of the stones upon stones beneath Nelson's Pillar in Stephen's *Pisgah Sight of Palestine or the Parable of the Plums.* Thomson's narrator recognizes the inevitability of the image, however, as he comes upon the frozen study of the "Sage" who, like himself, like Mr. Duffy and Gabriel Conroy, has rationalized loneliness of the heart in the name of knowledge, learning:

> The cords of sympathy which should have bound me
> In sweet communion with earth's brotherhood,
> I drew in tight and tighter still around me,
> Strangling my best existence for a mood.
> What—Solitude in midst of a great City,
> In midst of crowded myriads brimmed with Life.
>
> ("The City," XIX)

And like Gabriel, this dead visitor among the living accepts his metaphoric fate with a sigh of insight into the only, ironic, mode of union left to him:

> The flesh that crept like worms is growing numb;
> The raging fire of blood is dying cold;
> The rout of fiendish thoughts are almost dumb:
> The heavens fade like a Vision cycles-old,
> Where from dead eyes gaze thoughts uncomprehended:
> Thank God, I soon shall cease to be alone;
> My mad discordant life is nearly blended
> With all this realm's unsuffering death of stone.
>
> ("The City," XIX)

The last part of the poem takes the narrator back to warn that city which he had originally fled to be aware of "the burning fire of the law of the Truth of the Living God" (IV), a city that now clearly is a modern London threatened with the fates of Venice and Carthage in the language Ezekiel poured upon Tyre.

It will be apparent that the poem is Dantesque in conception. An allegorical traveler into his own heart goes half-literally out of his own city of sin into a city peopled with poetic punishment, stony metaphor of his own refusal of *caritas* or, as Joyce would say of his fabulous voyages in another city, of atonement, communion with the stream of life:

> Dire Vanity! to think to break the union
> That interweaveth strictly soul with soul
> In constant, sane, life-nourishing communion:
> The rivers ever to the ocean roll,

> The ocean-waters feed the clouds on high
> Whose rains descending feed the flowing rivers:
> All the world's children must how quickly die
> Were they not all receivers and all givers!
>
> ("The City," XIX)

Inferno, purgatorio, paradiso promesso: these are the stages of Thomson's early vision. But when he came to rewrite that vision in *The City of Dreadful Night* the poem was constricted within the confines of an infernal city, as its epigraph warned: "Per me si va nella città dolente."[10] "The City is of Night; perchance of Death" (I:1), it is peopled with flitting figures in the waste land, "as in some necropolis. . . . Each wrapt in his own doom, they wander, wander" (I:50–54). Their presence makes it a more terrible place than the earlier city of stone, a place more akin to Bloom's melancholy Dublin, with a "cityful passing away" always among the "Houses, . . . streets, . . . piledup bricks . . . worn away age after age":

> The city is not ruinous, although
> Great ruins of an unremembered past,
> With others of a few short years ago
> More sad, are found within its precincts vast.
> The street-lamps always burn; but scarce a casement
> In house or palace front from roof to basement
> Doth glow or gleam athwart the mirk air cast.
>
> (I:36–42)

When the narrator *does* see a lighted mansion in the night, he enters it to find that its lights, like those of the window watched by the boy in "The Sisters," are funereal: a young girl lies dead, and her lover mourns her in every room with the candles of the deathwatch (X). It is a city surrounded by a fearful desert (IV), its cathedral confronted by the impassive blankness of the sphinx. It is, in short, the living death of Hell, the Dantesque epigraph being imported into the poem to tell us that "They leave all hope behind who enter there" (I:78). It has been shown that the poem, begun in Thomson's thirty-fifth year ("nel mezzo del cammin di nostra vita"), was originally conceived as a first-person allegorical journey based upon *La divina commedia;* but when Thomson returned to it in 1873 he restructured it around a

London that had lost God.[11] The influence of Dante's fascination with numerological symbolism based in the triad, as well as the rationale for the "City's" fate, is epitomized in the following passage:

> He circled thus for ever tracing out
> The series of the fraction left of Life;
> Perpetual recurrence in the scope
> Of but three terms, dead Faith, dead Love, dead Hope
>
> (II:45–48)

to which Thomson appended the following footnote: "Life divided by that persistent three $=\frac{LXX}{333}=.\dot{2}1\dot{0}$." The significance seems clear: seventy years divided by this dread trinity equals a diminishing return to nothing. The modern Dante then, writing an *Inferno* without, this time, the promise of amelioration gestured toward in "Doom of a City"—that would be our sense of Thomson and his *The City of Dreadful Night* were it not for section VI, which suddenly makes Dante's book of the damned not a model but a mere metaphor for a more profound, inexpressible sense of despair reversing the relations of model and original: Thomson's "City" is the city of Night because Chaos, Hesiod informed poets long ago, is the mother of Night. A prophetic preacher gathers the people (XIV) to announce his discovery of the one truth, that Man is without meaning: "There is no God; no Fiend with names divine/Made us and tortures us; If we must pine,/It is to satiate no Being's gall" (40–42). The universe is unplanned, Night born of Chaos. And this discovery is that which makes the City Hell's own model. In the sixth section a dark form joins another beside a river. The newcomer has returned from a search that has failed. He has made the epic pilgrimage to the underworld, but ironically it is Dante's Hell, not Hades, he has sought:

> I reached the portal common spirits fear,
> And read the words above it, dark yet clear,
> 'Leave hope behind, all ye who enter here.'
>
> And would have passed in, gratified to gain
> That positive eternity of pain
> Instead of this insufferable inane.
>
> (VI:19–24)

But he is barred at the gate, commanded to pay in the least jot of hope and, having none, unable to beg the least amount from the damned, he is turned back to the City of Dreadful Night, which can now more truly than Dante's lay claim to the title of "la città dolente."

II

Most readers now are willing to believe that the gradually elaborated and expanded stories that became *Dubliners* represent a carefully orchestrated unity rather than a loosely gathered sheaf of glimpses into modern urban decadence. But the nature of the unity and the ultimate perspective of judgment it offers upon the society of Dublin are not agreed upon. And this is owing in very large part to Joyce's late decision to close *Dubliners* with "The Dead." Detached from the collection, as it has so often been in anthologies, "The Dead" has been viewed as the annunciatory birth of feeling as frequently as it is seen as Gabriel's epiphanic realization that he has passed through life without living.[12] The crux of debate has been, of course, the complex religious symbolism and the ambivalent shifts of tone in Gabriel Conroy's own assessments of himself and the evening's events. To argue a sense of the ending, we must, I think, work backwards and consider it as the ending of *Dubliners,* drawing the book together circularly from last sentence to first as we draw together *Finnegans Wake.* And to do so satisfactorily we must center *Dubliners* in that matrix of Dantesque cities of dreadful night of which Thomson's poem offers such a superbly sophisticated example.

That Joyce conceived the book as a vision of a dead "city" is clear enough from two famous comments: first, that he calls "the series *Dubliners* to betray the soul of that hemiplegia or paralysis which many consider a city" (*L,* I, 55), and second, he "chose Dublin for the scene because that city seemed to me the centre of paralysis" (*L,* II, 134). But there is ample information externally, quite beyond the precedents in late Victorian literature, to suggest that the infernal Florence of Dante's poem was in his mind as a model. Joyce's early study of Dante led him to tell Francini Bruni, "I love Dante almost as much as the Bible. He is my spiritual food, the rest is ballast."[13] And friends early and late, from Gogarty and Magee ("John Eglinton") in Dublin[14] to Wyndam Lewis in Paris[15] found it natural to see in Joyce "the Dante of Dublin." Further, the symbiosis of Father Purdon and Tom Kernan in "Grace" was, Stanislaus Joyce assured us, a parodic adaptation of the tripartite structure of Dante's *Commedia,*[16] implicitly locating the "pleasant and vicious region" that the boy narrator of "The Sisters" felt in his dream when he remembered "smiling feebly as if to absolve the simoniac of his sin" (*D,* 21). How much Dante's poem was in Joyce's mind as he was structuring *Dubliners* as a whole, though, can perhaps best be seen from the long letter he wrote to his brother in the fall of 1905 in which he outlined the order of the stories as he contemplated it in his penultimate version, beginning with "The Sisters" and concluding with "Grace."[17] He was at the moment completely obsessed with *Dubliners.* This same letter begins with a series of requests for detailed information in regard to several of the stories that he was clearly giving a final polish, and he had just written William Heinemann, Ibsen's English publisher, "I have almost finished a book which I would like to submit to you" (*L,* II, 108). He had also submitted "Clay" to the *Literary World* and was angry enough about receiving no response to write a mock prayer that, with its pun upon "comedy," psychologically identifies Joyce with Dante passing through the inferno of Irish stupidity (and how closely Joyce was identifying himself with his work at this point is clear from the remark about the early pieces being "stories from my childhood"). "O Vague Something behind Everything," he writes, "Give me for Christ sake a pen and an ink-bottle and some peace of mind and then, by the crucified Jaysus, if I don't sharpen that little pen and dip it into fermented ink and write tiny little sentences about the people who betrayed me send me to hell. . . . Whoever the hell you are, I inform you that this is a poor comedy you expect me to play and I'm damned to hell if I'll play it for you" (*L,* II, 110).

It was in this mood that Joyce had decided to conclude the volume with "Grace." Had he persisted in this plan, the book would have stood as a complicated parody of Dante expressing Joyce's disdain for a Dublin in which Father Purdon's religiosity was indistinguishable from Joe Hynes's patriotism. It would have been a parody on a large scale, like the "mystery play in half an act" in an early notebook that Joyce ironically labeled "Dr. Doherty and the Holy City."[18] But within the next two years Joyce's mood changed, and in 1907 his more developed sensibilities demanded modest emulation rather than parody of the great Italian. And in this new mood "The Dead" was written and added to redefine the structure of *Dubliners* as a whole.

III

The larger significant movements of *Dubliners* have been rendered familiar by a multitude of critics:[19] the boy at the beginning looks eastward toward Persia, the Pigeon House, Araby, while Gabriel Conroy at the end accepts the inevitability of his journey westward. The boy of "The Sisters" peers at a lighted window to discern an old man's death; Gabriel Conroy peers out of a darkened window at the universality of death symbolized by a boy long dead. The concinnity has its epicycles, too, making the progress of the first three stories a gnomon or *pars pro toto* of the whole. As the hope and spirit of childhood are abandoned to the paralysis of "adolescence" in the second grouping of stories, the lighted window of "The Sisters" is finally dimmed to extinction for the boy in "Araby" who "with anguish and anger" "heard a voice call from one end of the gallery that the light was out" (*D*, 35). Both the largest and the enclosed metaphoric patterns constitute an anti-Dantesque movement, from light to dark, as the *Commedia* opens in "una selva oscura" and closes looking into that "somma luce" which moves, in the final line and version, "il sole e l'altre stelle."[20]

And while "The Sisters" and "An Encounter" are stories of early summer (the one at the beginning of July and the other "in the first week of June"), the last story of the first group is set in "the short days of winter" when "Dusk fell" so early (*D*, 30), when "the air was pitilessly raw" and "the dark house" seems made up of "cold empty gloomy rooms" (33).[21] The epicyclic seasonal pattern of the boy narrator's dying hopes confirms the darkness pattern, moving toward year's end from its burgeoning. This is the more striking in that "Araby" is the only story in *Dubliners* in which the season is not appropriate to the protagonist's age. Those which Joyce called "stories of adolescence," "After the Race," "Two Gallants" and "The Boarding House," are all set in summer (45, 49, 63). The one exception in this group is "Eveline," which contains no indications of the season. But this omission itself appears to be part of the pattern. "The Sisters" opens with the boy speculating upon his relationship with the paralyzed priest who dies. When "Araby" closes upon its wintry darkness, the boy narrator has himself reached that "pleasant and vicious region" represented by the opulent "Persia" of the nightmare; and in finding that East the others had sought, finds it empty of hope or renewal: "Gazing up into the darkness I saw myself as a creature driven and derided by vanity; and my eyes burned with anguish and anger" (35). Following these words, "Eveline" opens with the first young adult also watching the darkness close over her world, but her quiescence is monitory of her ultimate failure: "She sat at the window watching the evening invade the avenue" (36). For all of Frank's efforts to move her, she is the most vividly, literally paralyzed of the long roll call of Dubliners whose psychic frustration parallels her own. Gazing upon "the black mass of the boat," she feels herself drowning: "Her hands clutched the iron [railing] in frenzy. Amid the seas she sent a cry of anguish" (41). It is the anguish of the young who have joined the priest in his paralysis, the "anguish" that burned in the eyes of the boy in the bazaar, but with the "anger" spent, all passion spent: "She set her white face to him, passive, like a helpless animal. Her eyes gave him no sign of love or farewell or recognition." There is no season attached to "Eveline" because Eveline is a symbol of the state of all the figures who follow, a state recognized by the narrator in "Araby": they are the paralyzed living dead in a dark world of stasis where change and movement are illusion.

Joyce spoke of the other stories as "stories of mature life" and "stories of public life," but one must not allow these categories to displace the fact that all of the protagonists in both groups are entering or passing out of middle age. In keeping with this aging, the seasonal settings are all autumnal or hibernal.[22] "Ivy Day in the Committee Room" and "Clay" are, by definition, set in October; "A Little Cloud" is in "late autumn" (*D*, 71), as is the break between Mr. Duffy and Mrs. Sinico in "A Painful Case" (112), while the latter's suicide occurs in winter (113); "Counterparts" is set in February (89); the events of "Grace" take place in a season that sees the friends gathered about the lighted fire (156) and the injured Kernan "huddled together with cold" (153); "The Dead," of course, concerns a banquet annually held sometime between Christmas and Epiphany (178, 185, 215).

The winter darkness that settles over the bazaar of youthful hopes in the epicyclic series when the boy recognizes life and love as the vanity of vanities is strategically positioned to prepare *us* to recognize the seasonal decline of the later stories as a dying fall rather than a cyclical renewal (although, as I have said, the stories are connected circularly, the boy of "The Sisters" unsuccessfully trying to conjure up brave visions of Christmas to ward off the vision of the dead priest, as Gabriel attempts to ward off the universal dance of death with the ritual of Christmas celebrations[23]).

These patterns can be discerned cutting a swathe through the entirety of *Dubliners*. Other internal echoings and positioning of stories, though, can be at least as helpful in revealing the movement and thesis of the whole. If "Grace" is a parodic, Dantesque journey toward the pinpoint of red light ("la somma luce") over a brothel on Purdon Street, "The Boarding House" (which would have corresponded in the first half to "Grace" closing the whole should "The Dead" not have been added), the middle story and last of those designated by Joyce as an account of "adolescence," is constructed upon a counter falling pattern into a modern urban *Inferno*. As a despairing descent from romantic aspiration into the death of Dublin it parallels the death of the spirit recognized in "Araby" (the final story of youth) and mocked in "Grace." Having gradually allowed Bob Doran to enmesh himself in an affair with young Polly, Mrs. Mooney picks a "bright Sunday morning of early summer" (*D*, 63) to close the trap of marriage for "reparation," a trap sprung to the accompaniment of the "constant peals" sounding from the nearby belfry of St. George's Church. And the way has been paved for her by the priest who had heard Doran's confession the night before and driven the naive bachelor so near despair that "he was almost thankful at being afforded a loophole of reparation" (65). The brightness of this Sunday morning is ominous, however, "promising heat" (63). As a naturalistic detail the phrase is almost refreshing. But the potential of a sinister underside emerges when Mrs. Mooney self-satisfiedly admires "her great florid face" (65) in the mirror as she prepares to summon her victim, a menacing image echoed in the companion piece when Father Purdon struggles to his pulpit, revealing in that particular inverted *Paradiso* for traders in souls and tea "a massive red face" (173). But, as usual, Joyce has sown the seed early. In the first paragraph we learn of *Mr.* Mooney, trapped by his boss's daughter and driven into drink and disaster as he "began to go to the devil" (61). Small signs, confusing little wayposts indicating the presence and direction of heaven and hell. Their purpose, I am suggesting, is to alert one to the Dantesque parody present here, too.

In "Grace" Tom Kernan (like Mr. Mooney, the Bob Doran of *Ulysses,* and so many others, gone "to the devil" in drink) tumbles into bestial pain by way of the pub urinal's stairs and, after his purgatory of rather cozy sickbed convalescence, rises to view his perverted, simoniac savior in the Jesuit retreat for businessmen. In "The Boarding House" Doran/Dante reverses the trip. Polly's "eyes which were grey with a shade of green through them, had a habit of glancing upwards when she spoke with anyone, which made her look like a little perverse madonna" (*D,* 62).[24] She had come to his room that first night "to relight her candle at his for hers had been blown out by a gust" (67),[25] and after that "they used to go upstairs together on tiptoe, each with a candle, and on the third landing exchange reluctant goodnights. They used to kiss. He remembered well her eyes, the touch of her hand and his delirium" (67). Doran has ascended into his fleshly parody of the Celestial Rose of light and love: "sempre l'amor che queta questo cielo/accoglie in sè con sì fatta salute,/per far disposto a sua fiamma il candelo" (always the love that quiets this heaven/gathers one into itself with such a greeting/to prepare the candle for its flame), so Dante had learned (*Paradiso* XXX,

52–54) when he arrived in his Rose; and it was, of course, at the third circle ("terzo giro," XXXI, 67) that he saw Beatrice, and, lifting his eyes yet further finally saw the Madonna, saw her in a delirium, quite literally: "E s'io avessi in dir tanta divizia/ Quanto ad imaginar, no ardirei/lo minimo tentar di sua delizia" (And if I had as much scope in speech/As in imagining, I would not dare/try to describe the least part of her delight, 136–138). "But delirium passes" for Bob Doran; as the trap springs he realizes the parodic quality, needs the powers of Dante's spiritual guides and transcendence to escape the lust he had mistaken for life: "He longed to ascend through the roof and fly away to another country where he would never hear again of his trouble" (67–68). But the mocking florid face waits impatiently below for sin's "reparation," and it is the penultimate hour ("it was seventeen minutes past eleven: she would have lots of time to have the matter out with Mr. Doran and then catch short twelve at Marlborough Street" [64]). Therefore, "a force pushed him downstairs step by step" (68). On the landing as he descends, Doran passes that hostile pugilist, Polly's brother Jack: "They saluted coldly; and the lover's eyes rested for a second or two on a thick bulldog face and a pair of thick short arms. When he reached the foot of the staircase he glanced up and saw Jack regarding him from the door of the return-room" (68). Christian and classic underworlds converge as, at the gate of a Hades that once seemed Paradise, Bob Doran gazes into the eyes of his Cerberus. Polly, above, has her vacuous "hopes and visions" (68). But Bob Doran knows better. Delirium passed, he knows heaven from hell too late, knows enough to relinquish all hope as he gazes upward from the pit: "His instinct urged him to remain free, not to marry. Once you are married you are done for, it said" (66).[26]

Twinned parodies of Dante's *Commedia,* then: the first, closing out the cycle of youth, presents a hopeless prisoner who mistook hell for heaven and (like the narrator of "Araby") was disabused; the second, closing the original *Dubliners,* presents a spiritual whore mocking the salvation at the center of "la somma luce" while complacently aging Dubliners look on. And these peaks of traditional metaphoric action punctuate the darkening and dying structures of the entire series.

The whole was recapitulated and humanized in that magnificent afterthought, "The Dead." From Pat Morkins's horse to Michael Furey the dead encircle the wraiths of remembrance who are the living; Gabriel Conroy sees his Madonna, too, at the head of the staircase, recognizing that "there was grace and mystery in her attitude as if she were a symbol of something" (*D,* 210). But when he and Gretta ascend their stairway to the heaven of lust the candle of love is rejected for a more truthful darkness: "'We don't want any light' . . . 'And I say' he added, pointing to the candle, 'you might remove that handsome article'" (216). What Gabriel is about to discover he has already remembered during his heady fantasies while "the morning was still dark" (212). Once Gabriel and Gretta were "standing . . . in the cold, looking in through a grated window at a man making bottles in a roaring furnace. It was very cold. Her face, fragrant in the cold air, was quite close to his; and suddenly she called out to the man at the furnace: 'Is the fire hot, sir?' But the man could not hear with the noise of the furnace" (213). One remembers that Dante's inferno is traditional, fire and ice, equally unrelieved and unmistakable mirror images of torment; too, one remembers that Dante paralyzed Satan in the ice at the nadir from heaven.

As Gabriel gazes from his darkened window (and as *Dubliners* closes), he sees the snow framing a collection of resurrection symbols: "It lay thickly drifted on the crooked crosses and headstones, on the spears of the little gate, on the barren thorns" (*D,* 223). But the icons of the Christian passion are as passive as the icons of his own passion when his wife falls into sleep with memories of the other dead, ignorant murderer of Gabriel's last dream of lust and life: "A petticoat string dangled to the floor. One boot stood upright, its limp upper fallen down: the fellow of it lay upon its side. He wondered at his riot of emotions of an hour before" (222).

IV

The boy's imagined "pleasant and vicious region," we have long known, was altered into a simoniac dream of the east, of paralysis, as the story in the *Irish Homestead* evolved into the version of "The Sisters" appearing in *Dubliners.* The allusions to "providence" were removed,[27] the boy was placed among the literary damned by his inability to pray,[28] the allusion to his unsuccessful "Christmas" fantasy to exorcise the dead was added. But the most important revision of "The Sisters" was the one for its opening, made probably after Joyce had written the last sentence of "The Dead": "His soul swooned slowly as he heard the snow falling faintly through the universe and faintly falling, like the descent of their last end, upon all the living and the dead" (*D,* 223). It is the Dantesque seal of translation that places *Dubliners* firmly in the Victorian tradition of "the hemiplegia or paralysis which many consider a city." Over the gate to Hell, Dante placed an inscription:

> Per me si va nella città dolente,
> Per me si va nell' eterno dolore,
> Per me si va tra la perduta gente,
> . . . .
> . . . .
> Lasciate ogni speranza, voi ch'entrate.
>
> (*Inferno,* III, 1–9)

Closing the book at the beginning, Joyce interpreted "The Dead" and *Dubliners* by unobtrusively placing the immortal phrase at the gateway to his own sorrowing city of the damned, by adding in Trieste an opening sentence to "The Sisters" which serves as an epigraph for *Dubliners* and an epitaph for the Dubliners we have encountered:

"There was no hope for him this time."

V

Joyce wrote to Grant Richards late in their disastrous negotiations about the publication of *Dubliners,* "It is not my fault that the odour of ashpits and old weeds and offal hangs round my stories" because, he explains, he was merely preparing "a nicely polished looking-glass" for his fellow citizens (*L,* I, 63–64). He was probably recollecting the "dark muddy lanes behind the houses . . . the back doors of the dark dripping gardens where odours rose from the ashpits . . . the dark odorous stables" that the boy of "Araby" contemplated (*D*, 30). Such descriptions of the sterile decadence of the city are familiar to readers of Dickens or Gissing, and it is this tradition that doubtless tempered Joyce's imagination. But because he was from the beginning intent upon portraying a psychological rather than physical waste land such as that which Thomson's despairing protagonist traversed, Joyce presents few such scenes. From *Dubliners* through *Ulysses* he chose to let a realistically detailed Dublin stand as its own denunciation. Aside from the passage just cited and Gabriel Conroy's very different last vision of man and nature leveled by frozen continuity, there is only one other view of the dead, barren city in *Dubliners*. But it is an instructive instance.

Joyce and Grant Richards had been struggling with mutual exasperation over deletions and revisions for nearly two months when, in mid-June, 1906, Richards sent the manuscript to Joyce to make what each hoped would be a final, satisfactory version. The correspondence suggests that this was probably the first time that Joyce had sat down to read and retouch *Dubliners* as a whole.[29] On July 9 he returned the manuscript to Richards. It was probably at this stage that he made the important changes in "The Sisters," including the Dantesque "epigraph," for he writes, "I have rewritten the first story in the book *The Sisters* and included the last story *A Little Cloud*" (*L*, II, 143).[30] And it is in "A Little Cloud" that the most sustained visions of a stunted Dublin waste land occur, as if Joyce felt that he had to "place" his volume in yet another way within the Victorian urban desert. When Little Chandler left work at sundown, he "walked swiftly down Henrietta Street. The golden sunset was waning and the air had grown sharp. A horde of grimy children populated the street. They stood or ran in the roadway or crawled up the steps before the gaping doors or squatted like mice upon the thresholds. Little Chandler gave them no thought. He picked his way deftly through all that minute vermin-like life and under the shadow of the gaunt spectral mansions in which the old nobility of Dublin had roistered" (*D*, 71).

Proceeding on his way

> As he crossed Grattan Bridge he looked down the river towards the lower quays and pitied the poor stunted houses. They seemed to him a band of tramps, huddled together along the river-banks, their old coats covered with dust and soot, stupefied by the panorama of sunset and waiting for the first chill of night to bid them arise, shake themselves and begone. He wondered whether he could write a poem to express his idea . . . he would put in allusions.
>
> (*D*, 73–74)

Chandler envisions himself as an Ur-Eliot, poet of *The Waste Land.*[31] And Joyce teases his own structure with the admission that he has "put in allusions" by titling the story after that little cloud no bigger than a man's hand which arose that Elijah the rain-maker might make Israel fruitful once more in spite of King Ahab's defection to heathen gods under the influence of the foreign Queen Jezebel (I Kings 18:44). Ahab's uxorious defection from Jehovah was, of course, repetition and culmination of that placing of the flesh above the spirit which had begun in Israel when his great ancestor "King Solomon loved many strange women, together with the daughter of Pharoah, women of the Moabites, Ammonites, Edomites, Zidonians, and Hittites; Of the nations concerning which the Lord said unto the children of Israel, ye shall not go in to them . . . for surely they will turn away your heart after their gods: Solomon clave unto these in love" (I Kings 11:1–2). In Joyce's allusive little waste land poem Ignatius Gallaher plays Ahab/Solomon to Chandler's Elijah. Returned to Ireland from such foreign fleshpots as London, Paris, and Berlin, Gallaher is full of tales of their immorality, tales of "when the *cocottes* begin to let themselves loose" (77), tales of "thousands of rich Germans and Jews" eager to marry him (81), and full of "many of the secrets of religious houses on the Continent" (78).[32] At first caught up with wonder and admiration at his former friend's glamorous life, soon Chandler begins "to feel somewhat disillusioned. Gallaher's accent and way of expressing himself did not please him. There was something vulgar in his friend which he had not observed before (76). As the whiskey warms the timid man to a sense of his own superiority, Chandler passes from his praise of monogamous wedded bliss to a challenge that is also a prophecy: "'You'll put your head in the sack,' repeated Little Chandler stoutly, 'like everyone else if you can find the girl'" (81). The king of the bedroom sought by those "thousands of rich Germans and Jews" scoffs at the prophet: "'But I'm in no hurry. They can wait. I don't fancy tying myself up to one woman, you know'" (82).

Righteous and defeated, Chandler returns home. Far from writing a poem, he has never even read one aloud to his prim, sterile wife, out of timidity. Holding his infant son in his arms, however, he now reads to himself a poem (of subconscious choice) concerning the death of a formerly beloved woman. He feels himself victim of an expense of spirit in a waste of shame: "Could he not escape from this little house?" (*D,* 83). Seeing the photograph of his wife, "he looked coldly into the eyes . . . and they answered coldly. . . . They repelled him and defied him: there was no passion in them, no rapture. He thought of what Gallaher had said about rich Jewesses. Those dark Oriental eyes, he thought, how full they are of passion, of voluptuous longing!" (83). In a barren land the prophet is converted by the pagan who escaped, but "he was a prisoner for life" (84). Then the child begins to cry, spilling ironic rain upon the land whose sin is infertility of the soul, and evokes futile tears of remorse from his father as the bawling infant inspires the one passion yet possible in Little Chandler and in his accusing wife: anger, not life. "Stop!" he shouts. "The child stopped for an instant, had a spasm of fright and began to scream" (84). But in replacing Elijah's growing cloud with these hopeless tears, the Joyce who renamed Gogarty as Malachi Mulligan could scarcely have failed to intend that this little story incorporate still another ironic scriptural parody that would take its much more serious, prophetic place in the allusive economy of *Ulysses.* It was the final assertion that the Dublin of *Dubliners* was the waste land. As Chandler/Elijah shouts at his son in despair, one hears those closing words of the Old Testament: "Behold, I will send you Elijah the prophet before the coming of the great and dreadful day of the Lord: And he shall turn the heart of the fathers to the children, and the heart of the children to their fathers, lest I come and smite the earth with a curse" (Malachi 4:5–6).

VI

Dubliners, the argument has been, was finally shaped as a barren city, an urban waste whose dimensions were extensions of numerous metaphoric traditions—Victorian, Dantesque, scriptural—all converging upon the single terrifying vision of Dublin as the modern metropolis of the dead.

But the same mythic visions of apocalypse had reverberations of hope which never surface in *The City of Dreadful Night* or in *Dubliners.* Dante emerges into a vision of light, a communion and community unimaginable in the cities of this world—perhaps his setting of that vision against the realities of war- and power-torn Florence is his deepest Augustinian commitment and debt. And Elijah's function, in the end, is that of a renewer, a fertility talisman to Israel disguised as the prophet of doom.[33] In *Ulysses* Joyce's emphasis shifted from irony toward acceptance of this promised renewal in his favorite scriptural type. The argument can most properly begin by reconsidering Eliot's *Waste Land* and the transplanting of the Elijah story into *Ulysses.*[34]

Eliot's introduction to his notes on *The Waste Land* begins with the assertion, "Not only the title, but the plan and a good deal of the incidental symbolism of the poem was suggested by Miss Jesse L. Weston's book on the Grail legend: *From Ritual to Romance.*"[35] This "incidental symbolism" is, of course, most clearly prominent in "Death by Water" and "What the Thunder Said," where one sees not only the pattern of the barren land, "the agony in stony places," but such details as the chapel perilous and, as the final speaker of the poem, Weston's central figure, the Fisher King. But the fertility pattern underlying the grail quest in Weston's reconstruction is superimposed upon a poem whose structural backbone is Dante's *Commedia,* the vertebrae showing through from the first vision of modern London ("Unreal City,/ Under the brown fog of a winter dawn,/A crowd flowed over

London Bridge, so many,/I had not thought death had undone so many") to the final review of Arnaldo Daniello's gradual purification ("Poi s'ascose nel foco che gli affina"). Joyce thoroughly absorbed these double structures of *The Waste Land.* He reveals this in a mocking parody that he appended without comment or connection to a letter written to Harriet Weaver; it is evidence of a buried concern with Eliot's poem that the letter is written so late as 1925:

Rouen is the rainiest place getting
Inside all impermeables, wetting
Damp marrow in drenched bones.
Midwinter soused us coming over Le Mans
Our inn at Niort was the Grape of Burgundy
But the winepress of the Lord thundered over that
grape of Burgundy.
And we left it in a hurgundy.
(Hurry up, Joyce, it's time!)
I heard mosquitoes swarm in old Bordeaux
So many!
I had not thought the earth contained so many
(Hurry up, Joyce, it's time)
Mr. Anthologos, the local gardener,
Greycapped with politeness full of cunning
Has made wine these fifty years
And told me in his southern French
Le petite vin is the surest drink to buy
For if 'tis bad
Vous ne l'avez pas payé
(Hurry up, hurry up, now, now!)
But we shall have great times,
When we return to Clinic, that waste land
O Esculapios!
(Shan't we? Shan't we? Shan't we?)[36]

To explain Joyce's obsession with *The Waste Land* and his clearly mixed feelings toward his friend's poem, it is useful to review a chronology. The "Hades" chapter of *Ulysses* appeared in the *Little Review* in September, 1917, and in the *Egoist* in July, 1919. In November, 1919, Eliot wrote to John Quinn about what became *The Waste Land* as "a poem I have in mind."[37]

Joyce wrote "Oxen of the Sun" between February and May, 1920. Weston's *From Ritual to Romance* did not come out until the spring of 1920 (it was reviewed in *TLS* on May 27). In June Joyce sent the "Oxen" manuscript to Pound, who was passing the chapters on to Eliot. And Eliot finally composed *The Waste Land* in the late fall of the following year. Joyce probably never read the Weston monograph, and certainly not early enough for it to have had any impact upon *Ulysses:* he knew about waste lands and fertility rites from older sources, as we have seen. Yet Jesse Weston appears more than once as a minor character punned into *Finnegans Wake.* This dubious tribute would seem to be owing to her prominence in Eliot's creative expropriation. It is, of course, the myth of Elijah. We have noticed that Elijah is implicitly evoked by the naming of Malachi Mulligan in the opening pages of this book about fathers and sons seeking one another for any reader alert enough to recall those two paragraphs added (centuries later) to the warnings of the Book of Malachi in order to give the Old Testament a fitting conclusion forecasting a second coming, a New Testament. Leopold Bloom is not explicitly identified as Elijah until the hints in "Lestrygonians" ("Bloo . . . who . . . me?") develop into the magnificent flight of "ben Bloom Elijah" into glory "at an angle of forty-five degrees over Donohoe's in Little Green Street like a shot off a shovel" (*U,* 339). But the point of my chronology of Joyce's literary interaction with Eliot is that Joyce apparently felt that Eliot recognized that "Bloom Elijah" had already appeared in "Hades" disguised as a parodic prophet like Little Chandler, yet one who would genuinely fulfill his mission as life-giver in "Oxen of the Sun." Viewed in the light cast from *Dubliners* and literary tradition, Bloom's Elijah-like role in these two episodes of *Ulysses* can usefully orient our attention as we read Joyce the novelist.

VII

The June 16, 1904 of *Ulysses* is oppressive with the mugginess of an impending storm. Bloom notices it early in his kitchen breakfast ritual as he projects his own sensations into his cat: "Has the fidgets. Electric. Thunder in the air" (*U*, 67). He continues to feel the coming storm in the afternoon as he eats and later in the twilight on the strand: "Whistle brings rain they say. Must be some somewhere. Salt in the Ormond damp. The body feels the atmosphere" (369). But the hours pass without relief until the sudden "smoking shower" that finds Bloom with Stephen and the students in the hospital while less fortunate Pepysian Dubliners scatter, "men making shelter for their straws with a clout or kerchief, womenfolk skipping off with kirtles catched up soon as the pour came" (390). The cloud that momentarily shadows the sun early on this particular summer morning culminates late at night in this fashion.

At the behest of Jehovah, Elijah goes up to Mount Carmel to herald the coming of rain to the parched lands of Israel, and "Behold, there ariseth a little cloud out of the sea, like a man's hand." That little cloud appears as Stephen on the Martello Tower parapet, like Elijah's servant on the mountain "looks toward the sea," and, by way of Yeats's poem, finds it beautiful. That beauty passes into a mortal frisson as "a cloud began to cover the sun slowly, shadowing the bay in deeper green. It lay behind him, a bowl of bitter waters" (*U*, 11). Hydrophobe, Stephen misreads the omen of renewal as a sign of death; this is not unexpected. But when Bloom, hydrophile, simultaneously views the same phenomenon, he too reacts with a shudder of mortality. Were it not for Bloom's experience, indeed, there would be no allusion implicit in Stephen's; the former event takes on meaning from the latter.

Through the serendipitous stimulus of advertisement, Bloom conjures up an image of fertile farms in Israel, cattle grazing, olives, oranges, citrons mingling in an exotic symphony of perfumes. This reverie is broken when he notices a street cleaner and makes a characteristic mental comment that sets an ironic context: "Watering cart. To provoke the rain. On earth as it is in heaven" (*U*, 60). Then "a cloud began to cover the sun wholly slowly wholly. Grey. Far" (61).[38] As this occurs, Bloom returns to his meditation on Israel, but with its exotic beauty gone.

> No, not like that. A barren land, bare waste. Volcanic lake, the dead sea: no fish, weedless, sunk deep in the earth. . . . Brimstone they called it raining down: the cities of the plain. . . . All dead names. A dead sea in a dead land, grey and old. . . . It bore the oldest race. . . . It lay there now. Now it could bear no more. Dead: an old woman's: the gray sunken cunt of the world, ...
>
> . . . .
>
> Grey horror seared his flesh. . . . Cold oils slid along his veins, chilling his blood: age crusting him with a salt cloak.
>
> (*U,* 61)

More ironically than in the case of Stephen, the Jewish protagonist, modern Elijah, mistakes the little cloud signaling the fertile rain as itself symbolic of Israel the waste land of dead cities: the Elijah myth has been invoked only to be again inverted as Joyce had inverted it in "A Little Cloud." But it is Bloom's inversion, and Bloom does not know the arc of destiny he must traverse in *Ulysses.* He is reading, instead, the book of nature, inverting to produce the sympathetic fallacy. As he circles Dublin's streets just after noon, the little cloud has begun to grow: "His smile faded as he walked, a heavy cloud hiding the sun slowly" (162). And this act of nature evokes that image of the barren city which is placed as epigraph to this chapter. But between the two clouds of Bloom's unknowing we, the readers, witness Bloom "succeed" in a promised parody of Elijah's rain-giving power. It is a parody, however, which not only invokes the scriptural myth but *Dubliners* itself in its allusive resonances.

If *Dubliners* is an account of the infernal city of the dead, the parody of Dante's tripartite *Commedia* within Joyce's modern *Inferno* is the story "Grace." It is the author's joke in *Ulysses* that when Bloom enters the world of the dead in "Hades" he should be accompanied by those same Dubliners who exhorted and escorted that other "commercial traveller" Tom Kernan to his simoniac savior: Martin Cunningham and Jack Power (the third party, McCoy, has already been disposed of by Bloom). But whereas Kernan is gathered to his friends' dubious bosoms, Bloom is more or less politely made by them to feel a pariah from entry into the funeral carriage through the straightening of John Henry Menton's dented hat. This chapter is the severest illustration of Bloom being an outsider in Dublin until one reaches the violence of "Cyclops" and his emergence as Elijah. Yet, cut off, he (comically) carries the promise always inherent in the little cloud. As the funeral cortege moves toward the cemetery ("each historic civilization . . . begins with a living urban core, the polis, and ends in a common graveyard of dust and bones, a Necropolis, or city of the dead"[39]) it stops (in mimesis of that "paralysis which many consider a city"), and Bloom looks out of the window to satisfy the puzzlement of his fellow riders: "A raindrop spat on his hat. He drew back and saw an instant of shower spray dots over the grey flags. Apart. Curious. Like through a colander. I thought it would" (*U,* 89). But it doesn't, of course, until night, except in this talismanic and momentary response to Bloom's little gesture of aid to the waste-landers. Joyce's trickster joke teases further when the carriage passes Reuben J. Dodd, usurer.[40]

In "Nestor," Mr. Deasy had assured Stephen that "England is in the hands of the jews. In all the highest places: her finance, her press. And they are the signs of a nation's decay" (*U,* 34). And his little joke about Ireland never letting them in is belied by Dodd's appearance. Passing the black figure elicits one of the cruelest scenes of Bloom's separation from his society, as he attempts to ward off anti-Semitic reaction by anticipating it with the story of how Dodd's son tried to drown himself for love and was "fished up by the slack of the breeches" by a boatman who got a grudging florin from the father for his efforts.[41] Bloom is rudely cut off by Martin Cunningham, who takes up the tale for Simon Dedalus, who caps it with his quick and cruel reaction: "One and eight-pence too much" (93). The whole is quite in the tone of the bedside manner of Cunningham in "Grace," as he authoritatively displays his ignorance about the papal motto "Lux upon Lux" and like topics. The caricature Jew ("a tall blackbearded figure, bent on a stick . . . showed them a curved hand open on his spine" [92]) is a symbol of the decadent commercialism of Dublin, as for Eliot's London. "Death by Water" is averted in the barren psychic landscape along the Liffey only when the passions of love are denied (in this respect, Dodd's son is trapped with Eveline, his frustrated suicide set in contradistinction to the passionate death of Michael Furey in the rain). But Deasy has been wrong about the Jews: Dublin's decadence is symbolized and participated in by those, "Gentile or Jew," who count "the profit and the loss." If anyone had noticed, it is the Jew Bloom who foreshadows the coming of life-giving waters upon the spiritual droughtland in his funny little wetting by the raindrops, the Jew who later will explain to the archetypical Dublin citizen that life is made of "Love . . . the opposite of hatred" (327). As "Hades" closes, Bloom emerges from the cemetery gates "back to the world again." It is still Dublin; he is cut off from his companions by the curtness of John Henry Menton, whose aversion for Bloom the latter interprets as "Hate at first sight" (113).

But if Bloom seems to live enviously on the fringes of the world populated by the Dubliners of "Grace," he is not without his effect. In that story they are judged by the merciless narrator: their ignorance is flamboyant, their lives shabby and their *caritas,* expressed toward Kernan, a parody of the spirit transmuted into simony and smugness. In "Hades" they are seen in the perspective afforded us by the narrator Bloom's role as a version of the divine clown whose divinity he is as yet only adumbrating, teasing us toward but mocking with his own misunderstandings. As he aspires toward acceptance as Dubliner, the Dubliners are automatically elevated to a status they lack in "Grace." Since Bloom is a figure of complex and mixed vision, the creatures of caricature in the short story must be humanized, too, as they interact on a new psychic rather than satiric plane. And their interaction reveals that for all the hatred and mistrust in Dublin, it is no longer Hell.

If Martin Cunningham seems the authoritarian bore of his earlier portrait in stealing Bloom's story of Reuben J. Dodd, when Jack Power begins to expatiate on the disgrace of suicide Cunningham diverts the conversation in deference to Bloom, knowing that Bloom's father killed himself: "It is not for us to judge, Martin Cunningham said. Mr. Bloom, about to speak, closed his lips again. Martin Cunningham's large eyes. Looking away now.

Sympathetic human man he is. Intelligent. Like Shakespeare's face. Always a good word to say" (*U*, 95).

Bloom is right. In the afternoon we find Cunningham and Power getting up a memorial fund to aid Dignam's children. Bloom awaits them at Barney Kiernan's pub, where he is viewed first with suspicion, then with rising hostility by a drunken, anti-Semitic one-eyed Dubliner (the "Cyclops" of Joyce's modern *Odyssey*) and his mongrel dog. Cunningham and Power arrive at the height of tension, and Cunningham tries to calm matters by preaching "Charity to thy neighbor" and concludes "God bless all here is my prayer" (*U*, 332). Nothing suffices, and Cunningham hustles Bloom to last-minute safety in the carriage that is both vehicle and tenor of his metaphoric mission:

> And the last we saw was the bloody car rounding the corner . . . and the bloody mongrel after it with his lugs back for all he was bloody well worth to tear him limb from limb. . . .
>
> When, lo, there came about them all a great brightness. . . . And they beheld Him in the chariot . . . having raiment as of the sun. . . . And there came a voice out of heaven, calling, *Elijah, Elijah*. . . . And they beheld Him, ben Bloom Elijah, amid clouds of angels ascend to the glory of the brightness at an angle of forty-five degrees over Dohonoe's in Little Green Street like a shot off a shovel.
>
> (*U*, 339)

Aside from taking a brief rest and recovery beside the sea, Bloom does not reappear until he enters the National Maternity Hospital in an act of spiritual charity toward Mina Purefoy, an old acquaintance who, Bloom has learned, is suffering the pains of a three-days' labor toward childbirth. It is at this point that the day-long impending storm bursts upon the Dublin waste land; and with it Mrs. Purefoy's pangs are resolved with the birth of a boy. But here ben Bloom Elijah as symbol and talisman of fertility begins the merger of metaphoric and psychic paternity which is the plot of *Ulysses*. The storm is announced with a crash of thunder—that thunderword of renewal which punctuates the revivals within *Finnegans Wake*. Stephen, afraid of water and of life, cowers as if under a curse. Bloom, rain-bringer, takes the occasion to comfort him and bring him under his own paternal protection as they move from this point toward that conclusion of *Ulysses* which finds them united, father and son, in Bloom's "Ithaca," 7 Eccles Street. Bloom, in the "myriad metamorphoses of symbol" which constitute Ulysses, is again the wily Greek. But the Hebraic prototype Elijah has, perhaps, not been forgotten as he prepares cocoa for Stephen: "What, in water, did Bloom, waterlover, drawer of water . . . admire? . . . Its infallibility as paradigm and paragon" (*U*, 655–56).

EXILES IN THE CITY OF THE DEAD

Joyce's schoolboy friend Constantine Curran describes a personal change in Joyce's manner between 1898 and 1899, the year of transition from Belvedere to University College. It was change from an ordinary boyish playfulness and openness to an aloofness that Curran calls "Joyce's D'Annunzian Mask" and that he attributes largely to Joyce's reading of Gabriele D'Annunzio's novel *Le vergini delle rocce* with its artist hero.[1] Curran has been alone in recognizing the crucial impact of D'Annunzio upon the young Joyce—an impact he believed was at least as significant as that of Ibsen at the formative period of Joyce's career. Between May and September of 1900 Joyce bought Georgina Harding's translation of *The Child of Pleasure*[2] and Italian texts of three other recent works by D'Annunzio, *La gloria, Sogno d'un tramonto d'autumno,* and *La gioconda,*[3] all this burst of book-buying having been made possible by the payment from the *Fortnightly Review* for his Ibsen essay. *La gioconda* had just been published when Joyce purchased a copy in May, and having read it at once, apparently, he dipped into his twelve guineas more deeply yet to take his father on a trip to London to see Eleanora Duse in *La gioconda* as well as in D'Annunzio's other recent play, *La città morta.*[4]

The interest continued. D'Annunzio worked at fever pitch throughout 1903: on April 18 he completed *Laus Vitae,* the eight-thousand-verse poem that dominates *Maia* and that was lavishly published a few weeks later; in mid-July he began work on the tragedy he had long contemplated, *La figlia di Iorio,* and he completed it by the end of August.[5] The play was published the following year, just as Joyce was in transit to Trieste and his Italian *vita nuova.* By December the Irishman was busy in Pola trying to find a place where he could review this new drama.[6] If he had also read the *Maia* poems, he would have found yet another view of the modern waste land in *Le città terribili* where the desperate dwellers rage and wander in cloacal overflow, soot and terror.

He didn't at the time, but in any event, Joyce had already come in contact with the D'Annunzian drama in the same tradition, and it had a large and lasting impact upon his imagination. In 1897 D'Annunzio wrote *La città morta* as a vehicle with which he could capitalize upon the rivalry of two great actresses, Sarah Bernhardt and Eleanora Duse, the latter of whom Joyce saw in the play in 1900, as I have noted.[7] Whether he had read the play by that date we do not know, but we do know that it was a book he owned in Trieste, because in 1936 he had Stanislaus searching for it among old belongings left there, presumably in the interest of gleanings for *Finnegans Wake* (*L*, III, 392). It was a book he might well have remembered over nearly forty years, because, as well as the open-ended psychic conflicts of *Exiles,* it suggested the structure by which *Stephen Hero* became the mythic novel *A Portrait of the Artist as a Young Man.*

In 1876 Heinrich Schliemann and his young wife, Sophia, fresh from the triumphant recovery of Troy, uncovered Agamemnon's "golden Mycenae." All of Europe talked of the tombs, which yielded royal corpses with their masks and body shields and jewels of gold, but it was D'Annunzio who made the archaeological discovery into a metaphor.

Perhaps remembering that the Schliemanns had been assisted by one Stamatakis, an ephor assigned by the Greek Archaeological Society to watch their work,[8] D'Annunzio peopled the Mycenae of *La città morta* with a poet and an archaeologist, Alessandro and Leonardo. They are accompanied by Leonardo's sister, Bianca Maria, and Alessandro's blind and prescient wife, Anna—a Cassandra figure serving to bridge the legendary past of the dead city with its present rediscoveries. The play opens with Leonardo's moment of discovery, and the trappings are all drawn from Schliemann's reports: "I don't know how to tell you what I have seen. A series of graves: fifteen bodies intact, one next to the other, on a bed of gold, with their faces covered by golden masks, their temples crowned with gold, their breasts covered by gold; and everywhere, on their bodies, at their sides, at their feet, everywhere a profusion of golden objects innumerable as leaves fallen from a fabulous forest."[9]

Anna's prescience is first expressed in an encounter with Bianca Maria. The latter, reading *Antigone,* foreshadows the plot by her admission that sometimes in this play she "seems to be reading my own destiny. I too am consecrated to my brother, bound to him by a vow." Anna demurs that Bianca Maria is too alive, too vibrant to be a sacrificial victim ("I feel in you a wildfire"), then mysteriously adds: "I am like a dead sister returned. . . . a dead sister who protects you against life from above. Perhaps I seem a shadow to you; I am in another world. You see what I do not see; I see what you do not" (1:3; pp. 31–33). What the blind prophetess and wife sees and accepts is that Alessandro is in love with Bianca Maria, a state of affairs revealed in act two when, symbolically acknowledging the sisterhood, Bianca Maria adorns herself with Cassandra's jewels only to be surprised and wooed by Alessandro while in this costume. It is an encounter that opens with their discussion of Leonardo's recent obsessive withdrawal into the excavation of the dead city and all its legend. And Bianca Maria's remark that her brother's eyes "seem to see nothing but phantasms" (2:1; p. 69) both connects him with the blind Anna/Cassandra and confirms her own sense of being heiress to Antigone's incestuous destiny, because Leonardo is about to confess to Alessandro that he has a wild passion for his own sister. The revelation is initiated by doubting insistence upon faith by Alessandro suggestive of the strange ambivalence of trust between Richard Rowan and Robert Hand:[10] "I have waited for you to speak for many days, to confess your pain. . . . Do you, then, no longer have faith in me? Am I no longer he who understands all, to whom you can speak of anything?" (2:4; p. 108). The confession closes with the tormented

Alessandro's plea for "silence," then a mime of the dreadful brotherhood of Bianca Maria's secret lovers as Alessandro turns away, walks to the loggia to stare at the stars, and then turns back to Leonardo; he touches and embraces him, and the two stand together on the balcony staring into the night and fate as act two ends.

The noose of insoluble dilemma is tightened in act three when Anna, mistaking the cause of his agitation, tells Leonardo of Alessandro's love for Bianca Maria; she then confesses her knowledge to Bianca Maria herself, making clear her intention to leave Mycenae and so sanction the inevitable union of the vital couple. Leonardo, wandering until dawn, reveals his own decision: "No one can go on living. No one recognizes anyone now. An abyss stands between us who shared a single life, a single soul. . . . There is no escape; there is no other way" (4:1; p. 174). As each participant reveals a quickening sense of crisis, Leonardo leads Bianca Maria to the Fountain of Perseus, near the palace, and drowns her for love as she bends to drink. Alessandro, following, discovers Leonardo with the drowned girl and listens as the delirious brother explains the triangular *Liebestod:* "I killed her that I might be able to love her again (purely); so that you might be able to love her in this way, too, before my eyes, you no longer separated from me, might love her with no more cruelty, no more remorse . . . for this, for this I killed her . . . oh, brother, oh my brother in life and death, reunited to me, forever reunited to me by this sacrifice which I have made for you" (5:1; p. 211). Alessandro's reaction is never known; they are interrupted by Anna stumbling blindly toward them. They try to remove the body before she arrives, but her foot touches it, she bends and feels the wet face and hair of Bianca Maria, and the play closes upon her uninterpretable (or infinitely interpretable) cry: "Ah! . . . I see, I see" (5:1; p. 217).[11]

For all of the Ibsenite dialectic in *Exiles,* the scrupulous meanness of bourgeois scene-setting, Joyce's play appears more radically D'Annunzian. The quartet of tangled lovers in *We Dead Awaken* seem focused in Joyce's mind[12] upon the extravagances of the crude hunter Ulfheim in a combat of psychic awareness with the intellectual artist Rubeck, and he clearly discerned the

Wagnerian nature of that play's *Liebestod* as the intellectual combatant becomes, in suicidal machismo, the strong man of the symbolic challenge to nature with which the play ends. And even in the academic context of death in *Rosmersholm,* the Ibsenite conclusion is, as always, the seal of personal apocalypse discarding with finality the rationalizations of an irrational world. But for the spectator of *La città morta* all is open: what has Anna "seen," what has Alessandro thought, what should we? This is the legacy of D'Annunzio to the insoluble dilemma presented not only to Joyce's characters but also to his audience in *Exiles:* "It is not in the darkness of belief that I desire you. But in restless living wounding doubt."[13]

D'Annunzio places his action within a second context that, in view of Joyce owning a copy of the play in Trieste where "A Little Cloud" was written, may also have offered him important suggestions. Certainly attracted to the notion of an existential struggle of the living within a "dead city" ("that . . . paralysis which many consider a city"), he would also have appreciated the ironic failure of response accorded a Jewish prophet petitioned by the victims of a Greek waste land.

The scene setting "in Argolis, the thirsty" is premonitory of a major theme. Again and again the characters advert to the dessicated state of the land: "this dry country truly has the feverish look of thirst itself" (2:1; p. 72); "everything here is dried up; wherever one looks there is thirst, thirst" (2:1; p. 90); "why have we come to this accursed place? Summer has burst upon us like an inferno" (3:1; p. 134). Alessandro even connects Leonardo's agitation to his long exile "in this country of thirst, at the foot of these nude mountains, closed in the ditch of the dead city, excavating, excavating the land, with those terrifying phantoms always before your eyes in the burning dust" (2:4; p. 109).

The proximate cause of D'Annunzio's play was a trip through Greece which he took in 1895. A companion, the painter Guido Boggiani, wrote in 1898, "On the basis of things seen in this journey, Gabriele wrote the action of his drama *La città morta.*"[14] But another traveling companion wrote that D'Annunzio seemed little interested in landmarks and ruins, being occupied with his "toilette, his suits, his shirts."[15] And D'Annunzio's own notebooks on the tour bear this out: a page was prepared for observations upon "Micene," but none were made, and the pages following, which recount the first days in Greece, are extravagant prose poems about weather and women.[16] It has been argued that in the writing of *Maia* D'Annunzio, wanting to give his Mycenean mythology a local habitation and texture, utilized tourist guidebooks.[17] The same technique was probably used for the earlier composition of *La città morta*. And given the archaeological context of the play, the inevitable guidebook would be Heinrich Schliemann's own *Mycenae*.[18] It was just here (if he was really as otiose in his travels as the evidence suggests) that D'Annunzio would have found a fact that he could translate into a mythic irony that Joyce perhaps echoed and clearly bettered in "A Little Cloud."

Towering above the ruins of Mycenae is Mount Euboea, which is capped by an open chapel. "In times of great drought," Schliemann explains, "the inhabitants of the surrounding villages are in the habit of going thither on a pilgrimage in large crowds, the priest leading, to invoke the prophet Elias to give rain."[19] D'Annunzio gathered Schliemann's sociogeographical observation into the matrix of his own dramatic waste land by way of its scriptural source (the source that Joyce would soon use so skillfully). As *La città morta* opens upon the tense dialogue between Anna and Bianca Maria, the latter looks across the countryside and informs the blind woman, "A little cloud passes, lightly [pasa una nuvola, ma è leggera]: a golden cloud like a wing. . . . But still not a drop of water falls. The whole countryside is thirsty. Yesterday a pilgrimage left Carvati for the chapel of the prophet Elijah to pray for rain. The dryness is everywhere" (1:1; p. 12).

The chapel of mythic hope is twinned in the Mycenaean waste land of *La città morta* with the Fountain of Perseus within the ruins.[20] Both are alluded to repeatedly throughout the tightening psychic developments, and they come together as the action approaches a climax with Leonardo's confession. Filled with premonitions, Anna and her nurse open act three with a discussion of the suicide of Anna's mother, who drowned herself in a fountain. The natural, if ironic, effect is to move by association to Anna's own fascination with the Fountain of Perseus: "We are all attracted toward it as toward a source of life," she explains. "Is it not perhaps the only living thing in this place where all is dead and burnt out?" The nurse agrees, asking only why they have come to this infernal land: "It is truly a place cursed by God. The punishment of Heaven lies over this land. Every day the processions go up to the chapel of the prophet Elijah. This evening the countryside is filled with bonfires. Yet not a drop of rain falls. You should see the river. The stones are as dry and whitened as the bones of the dead." (3:1; pp. 133–34). In these reflections upon the two symbols of life in the dead city, the ironic mythology of the play is epitomized. D'Annunzio's little cloud, like Joyce's, brings no life-giving rain. Anna should have known from her mother's history what the audience anticipates: in the dead city, in Argolis, the land of thirst, the fountain itself will only mock the living dead as it draws Bianca Maria to her literal death. Elijah is one prophet of *La città morta,* Cassandra is the other. It is her mythic destiny that is fulfilled, and Antigone's.

D'Annunzio's largely forgotten play may have stimulated Joyce's imagination to invert the expectations of myth in "A Little Cloud," and it certainly tempered the Ibsenite apocalyptics of *Exiles.* These would not have been large matters in literary history and might have passed unnoticed had *La città morta* and the companion novel *Il fuoco* not also shown Joyce the way past *Stephen Hero* to *A Portrait of the Artist as a Young Man.* In doing so, D'Annunzio's play perhaps became the most important encounter of Joyce's reading among the books of his contemporaries. It is yet another case in which history conspired with genius in the making of Joyce's art that this encounter coincided with the next great event in classical archaeology. And this conspiracy was augmented by D'Annunzio's own novel about his archaeological play, a novel that Joyce saluted in *The Day of the Rabblement:* "Mr. [George] Moore is really struggling in the backwash of that tide which has advanced from Flaubert . . . to D'Annunzio: for two entire eras lie between *Madame Bovary* and *Il Fuoco.*"[21]

PAST AND PRESENT

The Bridge of Myth. D'Annunzio, Crete, and *A Portrait of the Artist as a Young Man*

The "D'Annunzian Mask" may have been assumed in 1899, but the artist did not begin to surface until 1904. There are good reasons: the poet of *Chamber Music* and Dolmetschian lute aspirations; the would-be singer; the Paris trips; the score of pot-boiling book reviews. But, finally, in January of 1904 Joyce began to emerge with the notebook "Portrait" and the first notes toward *Stephen Hero*. By year's end, when he was in Pola seeking a vehicle in which to review *La figlia di Iorio*, early versions of stories that would be incorporated into *Dubliners* had been printed, and *Stephen Hero* was underway. The two projects, the Bildungsroman and the collection of stories, progressed in tandem over the next two years (the book reviewing, mercifully, had come to a temporary halt). The winter of 1906 and 1907 had been a hard time, with the disillusionment of the Roman banking fiasco and the subsequent retreat to Trieste. But out of the turmoil came *A Portrait*, as well as *Dubliners*.[1] On September 8, 1907, James told Stanislaus that he was preparing to rewrite *Stephen Hero* completely as soon as he had finished "The Dead."[2] By the end of November he had finished the first chapter of the new version and had begun to think again about the story/novel he titled in his mind and letters "Ulysses." He had an aesthetic quarrel with his brother-biographer which proffers the crucial indication of what was at work in Joyce's mind as *A Portrait* was taking shape: "On February 21, 1908, he condemned Bourget's attempt at psychology in vehement language: "Psychologist! What can a man know but what passes inside his own head? Stanislaus replied, 'Then the psychological novel is an absurdity, you think? and the only novel is the egomaniac's? D'Annunzio's?' Joyce replied, 'I said as much in my pamphlet.'"[3]

The D'Annunzian mode is set against the psychological. The stuff for the separation had long been in Joyce's possession, but, like later trackers of Joyce's development, the younger Joyce had been willing to see only D'Annunzio's mask, a posturing elitist making heroes out of a life that could easily appear laughable, limited as it had been to some forays among books and actresses, and a sometime seat in parliament. Then, suddenly, he discovered (perhaps goaded into distinctions by his grumbling reactions against Roman men with their *papagallo* posings which lace the letters to Stanislaus throughout the winter of 1906 and 1907) that D'Annunzio was much less autobiographical than mythic. And with this recognition of the Italian's source of vitality and permanence, Joyce discovered his own.

I

Let us begin with D'Annunzio's first mythic venture, the novel *Le vergini delle rocce,* completed just before the Grecian tour of 1895 which would inspire *La città morta.* Stanislaus recalls how Joyce had come upon the novel "and had been deeply interested in the imaginary portrait of Socrates in the first chapter. . . . The thought expounded in those pages is that the elect are those few spirits who, conscious of their gifts, endeavor by a self-imposed discipline to become the deliberate artificers of their own style of life; and that they owe obedience only to the laws of that style."[4] This aspect of the novel had to attract Joyce by elective affinity, but there was much more here which he only later absorbed. Set in Sicily, the novel exploits the background of a dying, commercial Rome fled by the artist for a more primitive

Eden of his youth. But here, too, all is lost, not dying but dead, a psychic state symbolized by repeated glimpses of "Linturno, the dead city." The noble Montaga family lives in memory of the failed Bourbon king of the two Sicilies and under the shadow of its mad maternal princess and its three virgin daughters, all dedicated to prescience of a mythic fate—a fate realized by the isolated poet Claudio Cantelmo, who observes them as creators and creatures of his own imagination: "Thus, at times, I believed to live in a myth formed by myself in the resemblance of those that the youth of the human soul produced under the skies of Hellas. The ancient spirit of deity, of divine nature wandered through the earth" (193);[5] "In her [Anatolia] there was a virtue that could have produced prodigious fruit . . . such as virgin Antigone appeared to blind Oedipus" (228). Himself imaginatively inspired by the image of his Renaissance ancestor's charisma, a charisma caught by the portraiture and homage of Leonardo da Vinci (50 ff., 525 ff.), the poet Claudio Cantelmo makes these maidens the stuff by means of which he will—recurrent words all of them in *Le vergini delle rocce*—"transfigure" the "weariness" of their own and modern Italy's exhausted racial blood, restore the "ardent" ways of the racial youth from which both he and his temptresses sprang. "All is death here . . . but all can suddenly come to life again in a spirit that may have a warmth and redundance sufficient to accomplish the miracle" (35): or so Claudio thinks, being one who believes himself "destined to engrave upon new tables of the law a new code for the religious soul of the people . . . while the presentiments of uncreated forms arose in me" (34). And it is through manipulating the buried passions of the sister graces, faith (Massimilla, the novice nun), hope (the queenly Violante stirring toward her high destiny), and charity (Anatolia, who protects her aged brothers and father in the shadow of the family's curse of madness), that Claudio comes to feel "upon the point of transfiguration, and that my desire to become a god was about to be accomplished" (192). The novel recounts, in short, just that symbiosis of "transfigurations" between the poet and the woman who is racial muse which Joyce ultimately refines in *A Portrait.* Claudio states both sides of this aesthetic transaction in one ecstatic contemplation:

> "Oh beautiful souls," I whispered to myself, measuring the visible rhythms of their existence. . . . "You are the triple form that disguises my desire in the hour of grand harmony, in you all the most stately needs of my flesh and my spirit could be gratified, and for the work that I am to complete you could become the marvelous instruments of my will and of my destinies. Are you not those whom I would have created to ornament with a sublime beauty and sorrow the occult world of which I am the indefatigable artificer? . . . each one of you will correspond in her entire being to the likeness that breathes and palpitates within me."
>
> (11)

But for all of his sense of being capable of creating a future mythology around himself and the sisters, for all of his realization that Anatolia appears "such as virgin Antigone appeared to blind Oedipus," Claudio Cantelmo does not write a mythic work. Nor does his creator D'Annunzio in *Le vergini delle rocce;* it is only a few years later in *La città morta* that past and present will be laminated, that Anna and Bianca Maria will relive the fates of Cassandra and Antigone in the shadows of ageless Mycenae. But in that play there is no internal guiding artificer, no theorist-surrogate for D'Annunzio.

Given Stanislaus's comment about Joyce's interest in the opening section of aesthetic theory in *Le vergini delle rocce,* it has been observed that "in the first version of the novel [*A Portrait*] D'Annunzio's is the dominant voice; but in the final version his tones are heard only in a few purple passages."[6] The first version to which allusion is made is the rather dithyrambic essay in the Paris notebook dated January, 1904. But if, in its "ardent ways" the dithyramb bears stylistic resemblance to the language and ambitions of Claudio Cantelmo, that resemblance has shrunken almost out of existence for the theoretician-protagonist of *Stephen Hero.* Yet his ideational alliance with the D'Annunzian poet remains in the minutely detailed account we are given of his "ineradicable egoism which he was afterwards to call redeemer"

(*SH*, 34). In *A Portrait* there is a distancing from the protagonist even as we enter more fully into his consciousness, a distancing that is only partially the result of the narrator looking back upon himself from a more mature vantage point. More important, it is a distancing established by the great discrepancy between Stephen Dedalus' sense of mythic destiny and our own. In *Stephen Hero* there are touches of self-irony: "The poet is the intense centre of the life of his age. . . . When the poetic phenomenon is signalled in the heavens, exclaimed this heaven-ascending essayist, it is time for the critics to verify their calculations in accordance with it" (80). Later, Stephen traps the president of his college into admissions of literary ignorance which nonetheless are accompanied by suggestions of the young scholar's immaturity: "The President's indefinite manner of closing the interview had left some doubts in Stephen's mind. . . . However. . . . Stephen himself, in default of another's service, began to annotate the incident copiously, expanding every suggestive phrase of the interview."[7] But such passages are lost in the sober autobiographical chronicle written not only of, but by, the artist as a young man.

Not only did James Joyce adopt the pseudonym Stephen Daedalus for his first published story, the 1904 *Irish Homestead* version of "The Sisters," but he transferred it to his surrogate-protagonist in *Stephen Hero;* therefore, it is not surprising that Stephen finds himself in both physical and psychic labyrinths. In the former, "As he walked slowly through the maze of poor streets he stared proudly . . . and watched from under his eyes the great cow-like trunks of police constables" (*SH*, 146); in the latter, Emma Cleary's behavior "led his mood through mazes of doubts and misgivings" (159). As a secretive artist, preparing his mythologies against these mazes, he assumes the D'Annunzian mask on which Curran comments: "He gave himself no great trouble to sustain the boldnesses which were expressed or implied in his essays. He threw them out as sudden defence-works while he was busy constructing the enigma of a manner" (27). Daedalus as D'Annunzio. But if the later novel will view the Icarian youth en route to becoming the artificer Daedalus in the formulation of an art, in *Stephen Hero* the duality of the protagonist will be more frightening, a function of the lesser narrative distance. The defence-work of a manner is thrown up not merely against society but against the mythic beast at the artist's egotistic center: the possibility of the spirit-body union emerging not as bird-man but minotaur. Listening to Father Butt's moralizing lecture upon *Othello* as a warning against the passions, we are told of the student protagonist's reaction: "The monster in Stephen had lately taken to misbehaving himself and on the least provocation was ready for bloodshed. Almost every incident of the day was a goad for him and the intellect had great trouble keeping him within bounds" (29); "The spectacle of the world which his intelligence presented to him with every sordid and deceptive detail set side by side with the spectacle of the world which the monster in him, now grown to a reasonably heroic stage, presented also had often filled him with . . . sudden despair" (40).

In *Stephen Hero,* as in *Le vergini delle rocce,* the mythic dimension hinted at is never developed to a resolution. Stephen Daedalus and Claudio Cantelmo both fail to rewrite the future as the transfiguration of the past. D'Annunzio learned to do so in *La città morta.* But it was only in *Il fuoco* that he would learn to describe the process, to draw together into a portrait of himself as a young artist the mythic tragedy of *La città morta* and Claudio Cantelmo's awareness of a mythic aesthetic and destiny.

A major portion of the broad debate about D'Annunzio's *dilettantismo* or *faustismo* has been carried on by way of discussion of his emulation of Wagner's total theater of music.[8] *Il fuoco* is usually described as a thinly veiled and self-aggrandizing fictional account of the end of the romance between D'Annunzio and Eleanora Duse. It is that, in part, of course. But in essence it is D'Annunzio's claim that with the creation of *La città morta* the mantle of Wagner's genius had been assumed by his own creative powers.

The plot is simple. The young poet Stelio Effrena returns to Venice to give a lecture in the great council hall of the Doge's Palace in which he will identify the ancient city of the sea with the inspiration of man's artistic instinct, mythologize it in the image of Veronese's allegorical mural of the triumphant queen which is at the center of the consilior ceiling beneath which he speaks to the enchanted masses. His poetic tour de force is concluded to the illumination of a myriad fireworks: his inner flame is recognized and imaged by the celebration of "the epiphany of the flame." He is surrounded by intellectual friends, most notably Daniele Glauro. But his real intimacy is with the older actress "La Foscarina" (read "la Duse"), whom he has prophetically renamed "Perdita." After a long platonic relationship as artists, their love is sexually consummated on the night of the epiphany of the flame. But on that same night, Foscarina has introduced Stelio to a mysterious and haunted younger woman, the beautiful singer Donatella Arvale. This seems to the older woman a willed act of complicity in her own tragic fate. She realizes an irrational truth: with sexual union her timeless friendship with Stelio will deteriorate under the realities of experience and age which separate them, and Donatella is destined to succeed her as Stelio's lover.[9] Donatella leaves Venice, but her shadow falls across the love of Stelio and la Foscarina throughout the balance of its history. And while the physical impermanence of that love becomes rapidly manifest to both of them, a new meaning in their relationship is reached when the actress's tragic awareness of the future inspires in Stelio a vision of the past: the vision of Cassandra which he will place at the center of a play about Troy, about *La città morta:* "And the still formless work that he was nourishing within him leaped with a great shudder of life as he saw the tragic actress standing out from the sphere of constellations, the Muse with the diffusing voice" (77–78).

> She had suddenly become to him very beautiful, a nocturnal creature forged out of dreams and passions on an anvil of gold, a breathing image of immortal fate and eternal enigmas. . . . The heroic fidelity of Antigone, the fury of Cassandra. . . . all were in her, living in her body. . . . Thus, with an unlimited vastness and through endless time, the outlines of human age and substance seemed to widen and perpetuate themselves. . . . The very genii of the places consecrated by poetry breathed over her and girded her round with alternating visions: the dusty plain of Thebes, the parched Argolide. . . . Transfigured by a dream. . . . appeared, receded, and melted away behind her head.
>
> (124–25)

So it is that a fictional history of the writing of *La città morta* begins. But if Foscarina is the Muse, the aging mother of poetry, Wagner is the shaping deity, old father and artificer of a new poetry. Paradoxically, in that it will be the poetry which creates the conscience of a Latin race so different from his own Teutonic myths: "Let us honor Richard Wagner," says a member of Stelio's circle. But in honoring Wagner, he warns, we must emulate, not imitate, the poet of the German people: "The theatre of Apollo, which is rapidly rising on the Janiculum, where once the eagles descended with their prophecies, must be no other than the monumental revelation of the idea toward which our race is led by its genius" (138). As he listens to this discourse on Wagner's relationship to the future course of Latin art, Stelio conceives his drama clearly for the first time:

> Suddenly, with the intensity of a feverish vision, he saw the dry, fated land in which he was going to place the souls of his tragedy; he felt all its thirst in himself. He saw the mythic fount that alone broke in upon its dryness, and upon the throb of its springs the whiteness of the virgin who was to die there. He saw the heroine's mask on Perdita's face, in all the beauty of an extraordinarily calm sorrow. The ancient dryness of the plain of Argos then seemed to convert itself into flames, the fount of Perseia flowed like a river.
>
> (139)

Later, with Foscarina, the transaction is reversed, and instead of seeing the Cassandran mask upon her face, he sees Cassandra through her: "The error of time had disappeared, the distance of centuries was abolished. The ancient tragic soul was present in the new soul" (191). And this aspect of mythic reversal is repeated as Foscarina visualizes Cassandra at the request of the poet, actually speaking "ex tempore" in *Il fuoco* lines that D'Annunzio had written in *La città morta* (347–52).

Stephen Dedalus' sense of what we might call his dual existence as myth and man is as relatively vague in relation to Foscarina's as is his creative development in relation to that of Stelio Effrena. Where Stephen's stirrings end upon a question, Foscarina's end in an act of willed acceptance. Compare:

> So timeless seemed the grey warm air, so fluid and impersonal his own mood, that all ages were as one to him. . . . Now, at the name of the fabulous artificer, he seemed to hear the noise of dim waves and to see a winged form. . . . What did it mean? . . . a hawklike man flying sunward above the sea, . . . a symbol of the artist forging anew in his workshop out of the sluggish matter of the earth a new soaring impalpable imperishable being?
>
> (*PA*, 168–69)

and

> Her secret life being in harmony with the virtue of the life which was being created, she was attracted by the desire of producing no discord between herself and the image which was to be like her. . . . The actress could hear the throb of her blood, her voice was to resound in the silence of thousands of years. . . . Your living soul [said Stelio] must touch the ancient soul and mingle with it into one only soul and one only misfortune, so that the error of time seems destroyed and that unity of life to which I tend by the effort of my art be made manifest.
>
> (342–46)

Her acceptance, though, includes a recognition that in the myth of the past Stelio Effrena's drama is a vision of the inevitable future. Leopold Bloom would later acknowledge similar patterns: "She longed to go. That's why Woman. As easy stop the sea" (*U*, 273); "If he had smiled why would he have smiled?/To reflect that each one who enters imagines himself to be the first to enter . . . whereas he is neither first nor last nor only alone in a series originating in and repeated to infinity" (716). There is a less stoic sense of love's losing mythology on the part of Foscarina as she contemplates the developing form of Stelio's play and realizes that the lamination of Anna/Cassandra and Bianca Maria/Antigone predicts and incorporates the roles of Perdita the seer and Donatella the youthful singer in *La città morta:* "Was there not also a virgin thirsting with love yearning for joy in the tragedy, a virgin in whom a great spirit recognized the living apparition of his lightest dream. . . . And was there not also a loving woman no longer young, whose one foot was already in the shadow, and who had but a short step to take in order to disappear? More than once she was tempted to contradict that resignation by some violent act" (343).

But she does not contradict the mythic fate. At the end of *Il fuoco,* Foscarina leaves Stelio's life for a tour of theaters among the "barbarians" to free him until he is ready for her return to triumph as Anna/Cassandra in a completed expression of Latin art in a theater that will be rebuilt from the stones leading to the ancient Janiculum. And Stelio/D'Annunzio realizes himself as the protagonist of his own play: "Have you ever considered the fat Schliemann in the act of discovering the most dazzling treasure ever accumulated by death in the obscurities of the earth for hundreds and thousands of years? Have you ever thought that the terrible, superhuman spectacle might have appeared to another, to some youthful spirit; to a poet, a creating genius . . . to me, perhaps?" (210).

This realization is set within a long aesthetic discussion Stelio carries on with Daniele Glauro as the two friends cross the Rialto. It is a night ramble of intellectual young friends which would have struck a resonant chord in the memory of Joyce (and may possibly have served as the bridge that justified metamorphosing the Dublin street nights with Stanislaus, Cosgrave, and Byrne into the aesthetic and spiritual excursions with Lynch and Cranly). Stelio claims he "shall invent a new form, obeying my instinct and the genius of my race only, as the Greeks did when they created their drama" (202–3). This mention ignites his imagination: as in a vision, inspired by the Teutonic innovator and the Greek spirit, Stelio finds *La città morta* forming in his imagination: "From that moment the explorer of tombs took on the aspect of a great hero fighting against the ancient fate that had arisen from the ashes themselves of the Atridae to contaminate and overcome him" (217).

The vision experienced, the artist must translate it through the ambivalent inspiration and instrumentality of Foscarina. As he tells her: "The greatest vision has no value unless it be manifested and condensed in living forms. And I have everything to create. I am not pouring my substance into hereditary forms. My whole work is an invention; I cannot and will not obey other than my own instinct and the genius of my race" (374). But as he goes forth to forge in the smithy of his soul the uncreated conscience of his race in new forms, Stelio yet has the encouragement of the great modern innovator of forms to express the conscience of another race, not his own. Stelio had watched the aging Wagner and his party as he rode with them on a public boat on the Grand Canal. Suddenly Wagner had collapsed, and Stelio had rushed to aid him. At a late moment with Foscarina, the memory returns: "The image of the barbaric creator reappeared to him. . . . he saw once more the white hair blown about by the sharp wind on the aged neck. . . . Then he saw the motionless body. . . . He thought of his own ineffable quiver of fear and joy when he had suddenly felt that sacred heart beating again beneath his hand" (374).

In the closing pages of the novel, Stelio Effrena is principal pallbearer at the funeral of Wagner. The bier is carried to a boat, and all embark: "The great silence was worthy of him who had transformed the forces of the Universe for man's worship into infinite song" (402). A service is held as preparatory homage before Wagner's body is taken North to his homeland, the bier strewn with laurels from the Janiculum. The closing words of the novel image the *traslatio* of the poet's laurel from North to South, from Wagner to Stelio, who will obey only his "'own instinct and the genius of [his] race'": "Noble indeed were those Latin laurels, cut from the shrubs of the hill where, in the days of remote antiquity, the eagles descended with their prophecies. . . . And they traveled toward the Bavarian hill still slumbering under its frost, while their noble trunks were already budding in the light of Rome to the murmur of hidden springs" (403–4).

II

Certainly D'Annunzio's complex interplay of autobiography and myth were attractive to the younger Joyce. The key word to express the artist-god's creative transcendence in *A Portrait* is that religious one, *transfigured,* which is associated with the imagined Mercedes, the literary heroine turned muse whom the inexperienced Stephen expects to encounter: "He wanted to meet in the real world the unsubstantial image which his soul so constantly beheld. . . . In that moment of supreme tenderness he would be transfigured.

He would fade into something inpalpable under her eyes, and then in a moment, he would be transfigured" (*PA*, 311). It is a conception of the artist's holy vocation as the vessel of language connecting transcendent and terrestrial, myth and mundanity, which was favored by D'Annunzio. *Trasfigurazione* is evoked a dozen times in *Le vergini delle rocce* and eighteen in *Il fuoco*; it is interlaced with the figures of statues, with the figurations of futurity in pagan myths, but is never more intimately welded to the poet-protagonist's own sense of destiny and history than in Stelio's sudden, ominous play with Foscarina in a labyrinth of an abandoned palace: "neglect and age had turned it wild and desolate, had taken from it all beauty and regularity, had changed it into a close of inextricable mazes" (283). Dead palace within the vision of the dead city. But while it becomes for Foscarina a secret terror, associating the rival Donatella with Ariadne, for Stelio it becomes a mythic bridge between himself and the archetypical artificer:

> . . . the wild mystery, the contact with the earth, the ardor of autumn . . . the very presence of the stone deities, poured into his physical pleasure an illusion of antique poetry . . . the spell of his imagination renewed in that entangled place the industry of the first maker of wings, the myth of the monster which was born of Pasiphae and the Bull, the Attic fable of Theseus in Crete. . . . The whole of that world became real to him, he was being transfigured . . . according to the instincts of his blood and the memories of his intellect.
>
> (287)

III

In retrospect one can recognize Joyce's excitement at and emulation of D'Annunzio's drama and the novel subsequently built from the stuff of his own (fictionally distanced) statement of an aesthetic bridging classical past and Italian present. It was a discovery fledged upon the wings of Wagnerian racism. But two questions tease imagination. First, why did Joyce elaborate the Dedalian myth instead of (as Stelio/D'Annunzio himself had done with Wagner) emulating and challenging its force in a more native context? Second, why did it take so many years after his realization of D'Annunzio's breakthrough to reorganize the autobiography of

Stephen Hero into the mythographic form of *A Portrait*? The answers to these questions are embedded in two bits of literary and cultural history. The first is minor, but crucial: the publication saga of D'Annunzio's *Laus Vitae.* The second was a major cultural event, the greatest archaeological breakthrough since that uncovering of Troy which had so affected D'Annunzio's imagination.

Coincidence surrounds this chapter of literary history, as it does so many that touch Joyce. D'Annunzio dated the completion of *Il fuoco* from Settignano on February 13, 1900. Less than two months later the world of Daedalus' labyrinthine[10] labors upon Crete had ceased to be mere fable and had become a fabulous history.

The story has often been told. In 1886 Heinrich Schliemann followed Thucydides' hints to Crete in search of the legendary Minoan culture, but he died too soon to unearth the riches his archaeological instincts had pinpointed. As a young man Sir Arthur Evans, who later became Keeper of the Ashmolean, had visited Schliemann in Greece. A decade later, Evans followed the late Schliemann's trail to Crete. In March of 1900, weeks after D'Annunzio's labyrinthine fantasies of *Il fuoco* had been played out, Evans unearthed the Palace of Knossos with all its evidence of bull-worship and ritual dance through the labyrinth. It was scarcely a secret kept for scholars. Evans announced his hopes in the *Times* on April 10, 1900, and a follow-up letter under the rubric "Remarkable Discoveries in Crete" was published on the eighteenth.[11] For a decade after this breakthrough, Evans's findings dominated not only archaeological journals, but popularizing vehicles as well: *Scientific American, Nation,* and *Gentleman's Monthly*, not to mention that *Fortnightly Review* in which Joyce had published on Ibsen's new drama in the very year of Evans's triumph. Typical excitement is betrayed in an *Athenaeum* article of 1902, the tone of which suggests why young Joyce might have begun adopting the pseudonym of Stephen Dedalus for letters and for his first story in the *Irish Homestead*: "The whole result of the excavations at Knossos has been to bring out in a remarkable way the underlying element of truth in ancient tradition. In the exquisite works of painting and sculpture which in certain lines carry the art of prehistoric Crete beyond anything that was achieved till the days of the Italian Renaissance. We have now true knowledge of what was dimly associated with the name 'Daedalus.'"[12]

Again, coincidence teases imagination, teases it strongly enough, however, to convince one that the Joycean "epiphany" was not a genre but a reflex rubric. D'Annunzio had subtitled the first section of *Il fuoco* "L'Epifania del fuoco,"[13] but Jane Harrison, in *A Prolegomena to the Study of Greek Religion* (1903), also had described a stage of the bull-worshipping dance on Crete as an "epiphany, outward and inward, that was the goal of all purification, of all consecration, not the enunciation or elucidation of arcane dogma, but the revelation, the fruition, of the god himself."[14]

Predictably, D'Annunzio was fascinated by the Cretan findings. But as transcendentally aspiring artist (Nietzschean inversion), he could scarcely identify with the old artificer Daedalus. In *Laus Vitae* he exploited a cross-fertilization of the locality, the sights and smells, the texture, of his Grecian trip with Ovidian themes. But it was in the fourth dithyramb of the *Alcyone* poems of this collection that D'Annunzio found his voice and persona recovered from the ruins of Crete: it was not that of Daedalus, but Icarus. In the extensive notebooks that D'Annunzio published as *Le faville del maglio,* he recalls the composition of the Icarian *Ditirambo IV:*

> For days and days the shadow of Icarus tormented and exalted me. I saw him between me and familiar persons, between me and customary things, sometimes with the projection and color of a hallucination . . . he was my spirit, he was my body itself; he was my suffering as a man without wings, he was my anxiety for flight . . . it was not he who yearned in me, not he who cried out in me; but rather I cried out in him . . . I battered myself like an ardent eagle in a blind cage. . . . The poetry made a knot in my throat like tears, like blood. My will to speak broke the meter, overcame numbers. Every great strophe of the Dithyramb began for me "Icarus said," it recommenced for me "Icarus said." . . . It was like an implacable breathlessness; it was like a yearning to drink in the air of titanic heights.[15]

The poem itself thoroughly bears out this close identification of the poet with his mythic persona. Two brief lyrics, "L'Ala sul mare" and "Altivs egit iter," serve as an introduction to *Ditirambo IV.* In the former D'Annunzio sees the fallen wing of Icarus and poses his own task rhetorically: "Who will reassemble it? Who will know how to rejoin the scattered feathers with a stronger bond in order to again attempt the mad flight?" ("Chi la raccogliera? Chi con piu forte/lega saprà rigiugnere le penne/sparse per ritentare il folle volo?").[16] In the latter, seeing the shadow of Icarus upon the sea, he addresses the "Despot" of fate, invoking this vision of "his ancient brother": "I love to renew his trials into the unknown. Indulge, oh, Indomitable, this my eagerness for the heights and the bottomless seas" ("Le sue prove amo innovare/io nell'ignoto. Indulgi, o Invitto, a questa/mia d'altezze a d'abbisi avidità"). The echoes are Ovidian, from those lines that Joyce would partially use as epigraph for *A Portrait*: "Et ignotas animum dimittit in artes naturamque novat." But it is clear that in echoing Ovid (*innovare, ignoto*) D'Annunzio is also challenging him with the modern mythographer's independence, possible transcendence of his ancient sources. Unlike Ovid's artificer, D'Annunzio's Daedalus is a worried straight man to his adventurous son, and one whose unsavory collusion in Pasiphae's lust is set in contradistinction to Icarus' godlike yearnings. The first two-thirds of *Ditirambo IV* alternates between two sets of scenes. In one the would-be lover Icarus watches his father and his desired Pasiphae in the process of constructing the wooden cow ("innaturale/opera," 334–35), watches the sacred bull impregnate Pasiphae, watches the spent girl as she "shuddering, felt living in her womb the horrible monster, felt bovine and human son raging" ("Sentiva nel suo ventre, abbrividendo,/vivere il mostro orrendo,/fremere il figlio suo bovino e uman," 444–46). In the other, Icarus in piety to nature and the sun deity both, struggles nobly with the symbolic eagle, killing it only that he may bring its great wings to be made over for his own flight by Daedalus, "artefice sagace" (280). But he watches Daedalus from a physical and psychic distance: "Not seen, I saw" ("Non veduto, vidi," X, 399). The history of Icarus' unspoken love betrayed by lust (one recalls how little Emma Cleary, unkissed, received no rebuttal time from Stephen's calling as poet) is overshadowed by his turning away from both the girl and his consubstantial father, Daedalus, toward Pasiphae's own divine progenitor, Helios. The final section of the poem rewrites the Ovidian myth. The old artificer has become technician, the artist has become the young man. Where Ovid's Icarus was a foolish child whose father fearfully guided him into the skies, D'Annunzio's Icarus is inspired with destiny: "My father awakened. I said: 'Father, now is the hour'" ("E il mio padre destai dal sono. Dissi:/ 'Padre, è l'ora,'" 491–92). As in Ovid, the father's hands tremble, the warning to keep a middle flight is repeated. But here Icarus silently challenges his father as he thinks, "At the first flight I will struggle with you . . . I will conquer you" ("Al primo volo/io con te lotterò . . . /la mia forza intenderò per vincerti," 505–8). He flies upward into a cloud; the wings dampen, the flight sheers off—but the odor is strange and sweet (551–60), and vision follows: "Then I saw nothing but the sun" ("Poi non vidi altro più, se non il Sole," 586). Falling, he has triumphed, burned into the sea of inspiration by the divine fury of Helios (one may be allowed to recall the paternal substitution of Bloom for Simon Daedalus in midst of Helios's "Oxen of the Sun"): "My courage seemed unexhausted because my mind moved the dead wings, the immortal soul and not the weak arm" ("Mi sembrava inesausto/il valor mio che l'animo agitava/le morte penne, l'animo immortale/e non il braccio breve," 602–5). Exulting, falling Icarus salutes his fate: "Helios . . . an offering is made to you of these wings of the man Icarus, there is offered to you these unknown wings of the man who knew how to rise into the sun" ("Elio . . . /t'offre quest'ali d'uomo Icaro, t'offre/quest'ali d'uomo ignote/che seppero salire fino a Te," 639–41). Then "Wheeling through the eternal light, I fell into my profound sea" ("E roteando per la luce eterna/precipitai nel mio profondo Mare," 645–46).

So the remythologized tale of Icarus. But it is made more than a postromantic *Liebestod* by implications to be drawn from the introductory twinned lyrics of "L'Ala sul mare" and "Altivs egit iter." These make the old story into a metaphor of artistic creativity, a reclassicized version of the fortunate fall, a challenge to old myths and old Ovid by the young Icarus/D'Annunzio. These would remain only inferences were it not for the final lines of *Ditirambo IV,* in which the poet speaks, invoking not Helios but his mediatorial youth, middle member of an infinite series of merely human inspirations that must succeed through daring failure: "Icarus, Icarus, I also would plunge into the depths of the sea, I also would bury my virtue in the watery abyss, if my name too could remain eternally imprinted on the deep sea" (Icaro, Icaro, anch'io nel profondo/Mare precipiti, anch'io v'inabissi/ la mia virtu, ma in eterno in eterno/il nome mio resti al Mare profondo!" 647–50).

IV

Sir Arthur Evans had given Crete a vivid life for the contemporaries of D'Annunzio and Joyce at the turn of the century. One evidence of this was D'Annunzio's own sense that if history was what lay behind myth, then the latter was not sacrosanct, and the former offered as free a stuff for moderns as for ancients. All history, by implication, became the piling upon which poetry could construct its piers, extensions overarching the quotidian. That, after all, was what mythology was, in the end, about: Icarian poets flying into the unknown to bring experience back to earth or sea revitalized. Or so young Joyce might have felt, reading *Alcyone,* while writing the turgidities of *Stephen Hero* and before having conceived the full structure of *Dubliners.*

And this returns us to the problem of the long delay in reshaping *Stephen Hero* into *A Portrait.* Supplied with a mythic context whose details would be widely recognized by a British audience from the turn of the century onward, and supplied with a model for a new Icarian artist-protagonist by D'Annunzio in his poem of 1903, Joyce did not decide upon the new mythic form for the novel until late 1907. The reason supplies a wry little footnote to the economic sociology of literary development and, I choose to think, almost certain evidence of the importance of "*Ditirambo IV*" to Joyce's self-discovery. D'Annunzio's publishers were *i Fratelli Treves* in Milan. In May, 1903, they issued the first section of *Laus Vitae,* titled *Maia,* in a limited edition. The edition was printed in two colors on handmade paper with allegorical designs and ornaments by Giuseppe Cellini, and it had a deluxe binding. At the end of the year the next two sections, *Elettra* and *Alcione* (the spelling was later altered), appeared in the same format from the same press.[17] These were scarcely volumes that would come into the possession of the impecunious young Irishman living on something near charity after his return from Paris; for all of his interest in D'Annunzio, they probably would not even have come to his attention indirectly. But, living in Rome and Trieste, Joyce would hardly have missed acquiring the first cheap, separate reprint of *Alcyone,* which was issued in 1907.[18] It was at this point that *A Portrait* was conceived. In his first conception of a five-part novel, the protagonist was to be disguised as "Daly"—perhaps because Joyce feared that direct emulation of D'Annunzio was dangerous; perhaps because he hoped his readers could tease out the structural aspects of the Minoan mythology without direct instruction. But when George Russell had invited Joyce to write a story for the *Irish Homestead* in 1904, suggesting, "You can sign it with any name you like as a pseudonym" (*L,* II, 43), the persona chosen had been "Stephen Daedalus." Perhaps, then, this prior territorial claim influenced Joyce to change his mind. The wandering and sometimes wallowing months that lead up to this crucial point in Joyce's artistic life screen a great deal that we would like to know. But the most likely guess is that, having been excited and redirected by D'Annunzio's remaking of myth, Joyce withdrew into some confessional within himself and admitted that for all of the highly visible Italian's stimulation, he was a minor classic, and James Joyce could become a major one. In any case, anyone who was willing to risk comparison with Dante by reforming *Dubliners* was not likely to be deflected from his new vision of the novel by a contemporary teacher, even a D'Annunzio. Especially so if his lesson was the catalytic control by which the mythic author could renew, *revive* the past in a sense close to a literal reliving. And at this stage, shared by D'Annunzio and Joyce, the mythic and the mystical come toward merger. But that is an issue for another chapter because it surfaces fully only in *Ulysses* and *Finnegans Wake.* And it could do so only after Joyce had worked out the elegant but simple syncretism of *A Portrait.*

V

The epigraph announces the hubristic aesthetic that is the subject matter of *A Portrait* for those who choose to remember its uncited Ovidian conclusion. "Et ignotas animum dimmitit in artes": "and he turns his mind to arts unknown"; so Ovid is cited. But Ovid continues, "naturamque novat": "and changes the laws of nature."

The hubris is both passive and active. It is passive in Stephen's days of spiritual asceticism after the retreat. For even then he recognizes that "to merge his life in the common tide of other lives was harder for him than any fasting or prayer," and this failure brought "a sensation of spiritual dryness," indeed, "the sacraments themselves seemed to have turned into dried up sources" (*PA,* 151–52). The metaphor for isolation which runs through Joyce's portraits of Stephen Dedalus from the hockey field to his assertion in Bloom's kitchen "that he was a hydrophobe, hating partial contact by immersion or total by submersion in cold water" (*U,* 657) is seldom used more poignantly than in this admission to a spiritual waste land. But the hubris is actively embraced, endorsed in metaphoric explanation of the artist's ability to emulate God in creating a new law of nature: In the epic form "the personality of the artist passes into the narration itself, flowing round and round the persons and the action like a vital sea." And in the highest "dramatic" form "the mystery of esthetic like that of material creation is accomplished. The artist, like the God of the creation, remains within or behind or beyond or above his handiwork, invisible" because his "vitality which has flowed and eddied round each person fills every person" (*PA,* 215). This metaphoric insistence upon the power of the artist, like that upon form in the fruitless Aquinian aesthetic that immediately precedes it as Stephen plays the callow artful dodger to Lynch's probings, masks the end of art by concentrating upon its means. For the final end of art is social, as

D'Annunzio's Stelio Effrena and every proper Victorian critic knew. If Stephen must fly by the nets of Ireland into isolation, paradoxically he must do so in order to change the laws that have woven those nets into the very nature of Ireland.

It has been variously observed that all of the women in *A Portrait*—E. C., Mercedes, the initiatory prostitute, the bird girl by the sea, Rosie O'Grady, and the Blessed Virgin—are laminated into a figure resembling a muse to Stephen's aspirations. But it is his country friend Davin's peasant woman who recurs to Stephen's imagination until he ultimately makes explicit her role as almost oxymoronic inspiration and object of his art. Davin had met her in the darkness of the Ballyhoura Hills. Thirsty, he asked for water and she gave him milk (a gesture to be ironically treated by Stephen at the opening of *Ulysses*). "I thought by her figure and by something in the look of her eyes that she must be carrying a child. She kept me in talk a long while at the door and I thought it strange because her breast and her shoulders were bare. She asked me was I tired and would I like to stop the night there." For Davin it is an anecdote; for Stephen a symbol: "Davin's story sang in his memory and the figure of the woman in the story stood forth . . . as a type of her race and his own, a batlike soul waking to the consciousness of itself in darkness and secrecy and loneliness and, through the eyes and voice and gesture of a woman without guile, calling the stranger to her bed" (*PA*, 182–83).

His own mother, Emma—they are rejected by Stephen because they have already been fouled by Simon Dedalus and other false priests, prophets, practitioners of spiritual death.[19] D'Annunzio's Icarus, one recalls, had watched Daedalus befouling Pasiphae before his own heroic choice of fatal but heroic flight into aesthetic immortality. Partly, even, it was cause for this flight. And it was, of course a paternalistic challenge that was Stelio Effrena's cause, that of transplanting Wagner's discovery of a new racial expression in the soil of his own Mediterranean heirs of the ancient myths of the Janiculum.

Stephen denies the rites of familial passage because the Irish past is that infernal *città morta* of *Dubliners* symbolized for the young by Eveline's brutal father and Kathleen Kearney's mother.

Dedalus the father and the matriarchal muse that was even then inspiring the Gaelic movement must give way to a new spirit through which the failed trials at flight could climax with that resurrection celebrated as end and beginning in *Finnegans Wake:* "It's phoenish, dear." "How could he hit their conscience or how cast his shadow over the imaginations of their daughters, before their squires begat upon them, that they might breed a race less ignoble than their own? And under the deepened dusk he felt the thoughts and desires of the race to which he belonged flitting like bats, across the dark country lanes. . . . A woman had waited in the doorway as Davin had passed by night" (*PA*, 238).

Flight, then, in both senses, as escape and ascent, dominates *A Portrait* as a heritage from its Ovidian origins, a flight through which the artist will imp the batlike wings of the Irish muse until, standing in the sea, she can transcend the sacrificial dance of the Cretan labyrinth ("Her long slender bare legs were delicate as a crane's") to become herself the image of that creative spirit she has received: "Her bosom was as a bird's, soft and slight, slight and soft as the breast of some darkplumaged dove" (*PA*, 171). Classic myth merged with Christian metaphor. D'Annunzio's pagan hymn to the artist retold and made to resonate against the sounds of traditional Christian imagery. With a bolder defense of the artist's benevolence, one bordering upon blasphemy, Joyce seizes upon a way to adapt D'Annunzio's remythologizing of the father-son relationship to challenge the most sacred paternity. D'Annunzio had rehabilitated Icarus; crossing the cognomen of Daedalus with the history of a young man, Joyce realized a medium for rehabilitating the artist and the spirit in Ireland. It was another simple coming together of old images, inevitable experiences. Flight, fall, baptism into "the common tide of other lives" only to reemerge as "the God of the creation."

VI

The quest begins with a disillusionment already internalized from the disappointments of the boy of "An Encounter": "He passed unchallenged among the docks and along the quays wondering at the multitude of corks that lay bobbing on the surface of the water in a thick yellow scum. . . . The vastness and strangeness of the life"(*PA*, 66). Stephen is seeking the imaginary Mercedes in his restless movement; a little later—at the Whitsuntide play—the imagery deepens as a mark of destiny misencountered: "The sentiment of the opening bars, their languor and supple movement, evoked the incommunicable emotion which had been the cause of all his day's unrest and of his impatient movement of a moment before. His unrest issued from him like a wave of sound: and on the tide of flowing music the ark was journeying" (75). Soon again the sea within rises in the torpid aimlessness of pubescence and by anticipation of destiny as death by drowning, neither yet recognized: "all day the stream of gloomy tenderness within him had started forth and returned upon itself in dark courses and eddies" (77).

Destiny misencountered only because the myth has not been rightly received by the imagination it impinges upon. On the flyleaf of his geography primer the boy Stephen had begun pondering identity through verbal flight from self outward into the cosmos above and beyond Clongowes and the world, "The Universe." It is, of course, the problem of a double self which D'Annunzio had encountered, too, with his Icarian fixation: "What kind of name is that?" Nasty Roche had asked (*PA*, 9), and Stephen spends most of a novel uncovering the answer through sea and air, flight and fall. Like his early counterparts in the boys of *Dubliners* he must escape the dead city, his island-marooned fate, by flight over the labyrinths of ritual—church, family, alienation. But there is the premonition that the flight is as suffocatingly sterile as the "common tide of other lives" surrounding him. The young boy's primer equation of self with universe is chillingly repeated in the older boy's "equation on the page of his scribbler" as he sits in the college auditorium hearing not the lecture but the night calls of the harlots in the labyrinths of Dublin:

> The indices appearing and disappearing were eyes opening and closing. . . . The vast cycle of starry life bore his weary mind outward to its verge and inward to its centre, a distant music accompanying

> him. . . he recalled the words, the words of Shelley's fragment upon the moon wandering companionless. . . . The stars began to crumble and a cloud of fine stardust fell through space. . . . It was his own soul going forth to experience. . . . fading slowly, quenching its own lights and fires. They were quenched: and the cold darkness filled chaos.
> (*PA*, 103)

It is the observe vision, version of that mythic destiny sealed by his name, the first psychic flight that will be repeated but reversed in the wild optimism of the diary: "Welcome, O life! I go to encounter for the millionth time the reality of experience and to forge in the smithy of my soul the uncreated conscience of my race" (*PA*, 253). But that vision must wait until the Christian surface of Stephen's past can be submerged. And it is a slow but inevitable progress. Fictionalizing the trips with his father to England to see D'Annunzio's plays, trips made possible by the money from the Ibsen essay in *Fortnightly*, Joyce has Stephen splurge upon loans and treats in a fruitless attempt to merge with his family:

> How foolish his aim had been! He had tried to build a breakwater of order and elegance against the sordid tide of life without him and to dam . . . the powerful recurrence of the tides within him. Useless. From without as from within the water had flowed over his bar-iers. . . . He saw clearly . . . his own futile isolation. . . . He felt that he was hardly of the one blood with them but stood to them rather in the mystical kinship of fosterage, foster child and foster brother.
> (*PA*, 98)

The waters rise into daydreams of universal deluge during the retreat sermon (*PA*, 117), particularize as the Jesuit director offers the temptation to a false vocation. The visceral response is that of Icarus: "His lungs dilated and sank as if he were inhaling a warm moist unsustaining air and he smelt again the warm moist air which hung in the bath in Clongowes above the sluggish turf-coloured water" (161). It is the turning point, seen by Stephen as resigned acceptance of man's estate of inevitable sin and loss, but actually serving as prelude to recognition of his mythic role: "The snares of the world were its ways of sin. He would fall. He had not yet fallen but he would fall silently, in an instant. . . . and he felt the silent lapse of his soul, as it would be at some instant to come, falling, falling, but not yet fallen, still unfallen, but about to fall" (162). He crosses the bridge over the Tolka with irrevocable steps, leaving behind the priesthood and the Christian imagery in a last ironic lamination with the pagan as he enters finally into acceptance of his siblings to recollections of Newman upon Virgil, "*giving utterance, like the voice of Nature herself, to that pain and weariness yet hope of better things which has been the experience of her children in every time.*" A transition, then, a conscious motion toward that fall into the tide of life which alone can validate the poet as savior of his race: "They would sing so for hours . . . till the last pale light died down on the horizon, till the first dark nightclouds came forth and night fell" (163).

A darkness, though, before the mythic dawning of the burden of his strange name: the next section opens: "He could wait no longer" (*PA*, 164). He does not have to. Having passed the Christian Brothers on that second-stage bridge beyond the church, Stephen encounters his acquaintances, who shamelessly hail him in the Greek epithets of the sacrificial bull, which return the mythology openly to Crete.[20] And open its import to Stephen himself at last:

> Now, as never before, his strange name seemed to him a prophecy. So timeless seemed the grey warm air, so fluid and impersonal his own mood, that all ages were as one to him. . . . at the name of the fabulous artificer, he seemed to hear the noise of dim waves and to see a winged form flying above the waves and slowly climbing the air. . . . a hawklike man flying sunward above the sea, a prophecy of the end he had been born to serve. . . . His heart trembled in an ecstasy of fear and his soul was in flight.
>
> (*PA*, 168–69)

From Christian to classic, from the timid presence of the young man to the heritage of the father—but a cry from one of the boys warns even at this juncture: "O, Cripes, I'm drownded" (169).

The bird-girl/muse is immediately encountered, an inevitable presence upon Stephen's mythic mind, virgin crane dancer from the Cretan labyrinth, Christian spiritual dove. But a hoyden, too. If Stephen sees her "gaze, without shame or wantoness" it is because his own ecstasy misses the boldness of her hoisted skirts.

A structure of triple vision, then. D'Annunzio had allowed Stelio Effrena to adapt the *città morta* to a humorless vision of the artist's calling as a visionary savior of his race. Joyce learned from this a way to raise *Stephen Hero* beyond the limitations set upon the Bildungsroman of the artist from Goethe to Gissing. And, like D'Annunzio, he leaned upon the wide public notice of the Cretan discoveries which fed new life into Ovid's tale of a flight-borne father and son, even adapting D'Annunzio's retelling in which the son's fall is reshaped into an act of immortality. But that was D'Annunzio's assertion; Joyce validated it with the Christian imagery of a fortunate fall, vitalizing that with the reluctant artist's necessity to immerse, even submerge, himself in the tide of Irish life. A more careful weaver of mythic tapestries, the young Joyce was also a soberer analyst of his own artistic hopes and stance. Stephen Dedalus is no Hero. He has a destiny, but no achievement. He aspires to renew the Irish imagination, but he is no rival to Wagner. Indeed, he is a withdrawn young man with nothing mythic but a strange name: "A sense of fear of the unknown moved in the heart of his weariness, a fear of symbols and portents, of the hawklike man whose name he bore soaring out of his captivity on osierwoven wings, of Thoth, the god of writers" (*PA,* 225). D'Annunzio's romantic hubris is translated by Joyce into the ironic, antiheroic vision of a destiny that man cannot and must fulfill as his challenge to the old paternal gods. If his protagonist goes to forge the conscience of his race, he is a callow boy calling yet upon the deity he has rejected in a Christian context only to emulate and need him in another, both earlier and later in its import: "Old father, old artificer, stand me now and ever in good stead" (*PA,* 253). It will not be an easy or unerring ascent. In *Ulysses* Stephen will admit that, having flown by the nets of Ireland to Paris, he fell uttering the same cry for help from the past: "Paris and back. Lapwing. Icarus. *Pater, ait.* Seabedabbled, fallen, weltering" (*U,* 208). But now the triple lamination of classic, Christian, and contemporary will be joined by a fourth structure of family and fall by which the bitter waters will be sweetened.

IV

ULYSSES
Joyce's Kabbalah

One does not become a child of nature in the nineteenth century by attempting to eschew culture; one becomes, in so far as he fails, a *literary* version of the child of nature; and, in so far as he succeeds, a creature of sub-culture: of the world of "cosmic consciousness" and phrenology that lurks beneath the surface of ideas proper.

Leslie Fiedler, "Images of Walt Whitman"

. . . he began to sketch out schemes for Eleusinian rites. . . . The other world put all his magical knowledge into it, and into the teaching that was given to the initiates, and more would come to them, in dreams and visions as they worked. . . . He opened a large box, and showed Michael a rather battered theatrical crown and an ermine coat. It was a costume he had had years ago when he had played a king in some amateur theatricals. He said, "I will show you now what has brought everything about. . . . Sometimes I put on this ermine coat and this crown, and I kneel down and French kneels beside me, and I imagine that he is Melchior and I imagine upon the other side of me Balthasar, and I look over towards where that curtain makes a dim place, and there I see the cradle and the manger, and that is the way we say our prayers, and sometimes it all becomes so clear that I smell the myrrh and frankincense. Now I have the reward. The great change has come into the world again."

William Butler Yeats, *The Speckled Bird*

"Once or twice he dictated a bit of *Finnegans Wake* to Beckett . . . in the middle of one such session there was a knock at the door which Beckett didn't hear. Joyce said, 'Come in,' and Beckett wrote it down. Afterwards, he read back what he had written and Joyce said, 'What's that "Come in"?' 'Yes, you said that,' said Beckett. Joyce thought for a moment, then said, 'Let it stand.' He was quite willing to accept coincidence as his collaborator."[1] Even if apocryphal, it is a telling anecdote around whose edges peeps an immense mystical and personalized metaphysic.

It was a metaphysic born of reflex yearnings in the European imagination left frustrated by the peculiarly nineteenth-century version of the disappearance of God which had denatured Judaic-Christian religion into something almost as impersonal and timeless as yet another savage source for *The Golden Bough.* One road to recovery taken by many was the humanization of science into the political sociology of Marxism and lesser utopian socialisms. Their appeal was above all a restoration of the unimaginative; as clearly as in the medieval allegory, Mankind and Everyman became identical within a structure of projected predictabilities. Another principal way was the elitist gamble of mysticism. Like *The Golden Bough,* or like the structuralism of Marxists, modern mysticism has often been nurtured by a sophisticated historical syncretism. What it has offered the modern imagination has been unmediated access to its own structures. If modern intellectuals and artists more often have taken the first route, probably few have not been tempted by the other. The German cultural philosopher Walter Benjamin can serve as epitome of this phenomenon as a consequence of his indirect but deep involvement with the stuff and themes of *Ulysses.*

Under the influence of the activist actress Asja Lacis, of the work of Georg Lukacs, and of his Russian travels, Benjamin became a Marxist and established his long and fruitful friendship with Brecht. He never became a Communist Party member, though, and his work moved toward language theory rooted in a fascination with biblical texts. But going beyond Mallarmé's awareness of the protean physicalities of the book, Benjamin too redefined the nature of texts long before contemporary structural poetics. As an acute interpreter says in summary of his "city" essays of the 1920s and 1930s, "Benjamin, in an age without magic, continues to 'read' things, cities, social institutions as if they were sacred texts."[2] Benjamin's "cities"—Naples, Berlin, Moscow, in the early twentieth century—are perceived in the same perspective as newspapers or epic theater, by way of "a procedure that has become familiar to you in recent years from film and radio, press and photography. I am speaking of the procedure of montage: the superimposed element interrupts the context in which it is inserted."[3] Readers of *Ulysses* will immediately recall "Aeolus." But that "modernist" chapter centers upon Moses, and Benjamin's sense of text and exegesis came not from Brecht, but from the other friend and stimulus of his thought, Gershom Scholem. In the 1920s Scholem urged Benjamin to intensify his Hebrew studies with a view to recruiting him as a colleague who would be a co-worker at Jerusalem in Scholem's own intensive study of the kabbalistic texts, touchstone of ancient Jewish mysticism. Benjamin, torn between sociological and mystic roads past Calvary, turned his talmudic instincts in the direction of an imaginative semiology. But Scholem continues even now to explore the Hebraic texts most central to the mystic element among Joyce's contemporaries, central to *Ulysses* itself. Much of what follows is a guided tour through some of the more significant narrative and interpretive consequences of that mysticism for Joyce's novel.

But first one must address the larger question raised by Fiedler's observation that I have used as chapter epigraph. It forces to the surface that most elusive and unavoidable problem of *Ulysses* and *Finnegans Wake,* the relations between Joyce and his narrator (which is to say, Joyce and style) and between Joyce and his alter egos, who are, as a less sophisticated critical age rightly assumed, Stephen Dedalus and Shem the Penman. If *Ulysses* is to be seen seriously as Joyce's kabbalah, one can seriously ask in what sense its author was a mystic, as its protagonist is a Jew.

I. *The Psycho-Biography of James the Penman*

"James Joyce":

The name of Joyce is derived by genealogists from the French *joyeux* and the Latin *jocax,* and James Joyce, who held that literature

> should express the "holy spirit of joy," accepted his name as an omen. In later life he carried a seventeenth-century picture of a Duc de Joyeux in his wallet. . . . On the other hand, he enjoyed referring to himself as "James Joyless," "a Joyce in the wilderness," "a Joyce of evil," and considered Freud a namesake, though an undesired one.[4]

Born Rapagnetta, Joyce's mythic mentor not only called himself but became in his aesthetic and political life Gabriele D'Annunzio, angel of the annunciation, living expression of a second coming, but yet able to project himself into that new Icarus of the *Maia* poems, to *breathe* in the sea through the falling hero-poet he recreated from the myth. Joyce, as we have seen, emulated by early adapting the artificer's name as his own. The historical speculations in the last chapter may suffice to explain the transference that became itself a structural principle in *A Portrait.* But they do nothing to explain why Stephen Dedalus should have to return in *Ulysses* with—as mocking Mulligan points out—"Your absurd name, an ancient Greek" emphasized at the very beginning (*U,* 4). The genesis of this lies not in the structural continuity between the two fictions (the continuities, simple and infrequent, are on narrative surfaces), but in the author's sense of himself as a bridge between the two, between the fictions and earlier myth, between the fictions and his personal role as that author whose art was divinely creative in that (recalling the Ovidian epigraph to *A Portrait*) it would remake the nature of the Irish psyche in the image of his own.

As we have realized with a variety of profitable commentators, *Ulysses* is an older man's book, written by and largely about a father, and Bloom is in many respects a Joycean avatar as much as is Stephen. An Irish mythology, the earlier one in *A Portrait,* featuring a young Greek, might echo and honor some of the pride taken in the Grecian origins of the Irish race (origins emphasized not only by Bérard but by that other coincidental namesake, P. W. Joyce).[5] And Bloom's heritage could emanate not only from the Mosaic translation of a people oppressed, like the Irish, beyond the reach of the Pharoahs, but also from that triumph of liberation from the Austrian Empire which Arthur Griffith set forth as model for the Irish independents in *The Resurrection of Hungary* (1904).[6] But this leaves us the particular of Bloom's name, caught up in a pattern that insists upon allegory somewhere beyond mere metaphors: Virag, the pseudonym Henry Flower, the other father Nestor-Deasy, the recurrent roses, the closure upon Molly as "my mountain flower." It is a particular not unrelated to the new avatar Joyce chose for the writer in *Finnegans Wake*: Shem the Penman.

Ellman remarks that Joyce's fictional method "is not a perception of order or of love; . . . it is the perception of coincidence."[7] On the night of his fortieth birthday, the night of the publication of *Ulysses*, Joyce "pointed out a coincidence, as he was to do more and more often for the rest of his life, this time the fact that he had mentioned the name of the Duke of Tetuan and that the present Duke was at that moment in Paris at the Irish convention. His feeling of the book's prophetic and magical nature seized upon every corroboration."[8] The "perception of coincidence" escalated as a matter of course in the *Wake*, as with the geneses of Earwicker's sons: "Shem and Shaun, were based in part upon two feeble-minded hangers-on, James and John Ford, who lived in Dublin on the North Strand. They were known as 'Shem and Shaun,' and were famous for their incomprehensible speech and their shuffling gait. . . . Of course, Joyce had for models also himself and his brother *John* Stanislaus Joyce, Jr. But . . . he had in mind also *Jim the Penman*, a play about a forger by Sir Charles Young."[9]

Forging and forgery as descriptions of opposing but symbiotic aspects of authorial creation had been in Joyce's mind since the conclusion of *A Portrait* where the young artist going forth to forge a new Irish consciousness wears the prematurely borrowed robes of Daedalus, the mythic artificer. In *Finnegans Wake* that forgery is compounded as the author of "the uselessly unreadable Blue Book of Eccles" (*FW*, 179) written from his own excrement turns out to be Shem, who "was a sham and a low sham" (170). Like Captain O'Shea at Parnell's trial, party to a forgery again from his own wasted life stuff, "every day in everyone's way more exceeding in violent abuse of self and others," Shem lived in "the house O'Shea or O'Shame . . . known as the Haunted Inkbottle, no number Brimstone Walk, . . . with his penname SHUT sepia-scraped on the doorplate" (182–83). Little wonder that brother Justius can conclude for silence, "Sh! Shem, you are. Sh! You are mad!" (193).[10]

But the final "coincidence" of name and theme arises certainly as fount for all the lesser convergences from that source which is itself the divine joke book for all the wildly improbable puns of holy writ, the kabbalistic *Sepher ha Zohar.* Here the letters of the Hebrew alphabet offer themselves in order before God for the job of creation. Shin [ש] has all the doubleness of his namesake Shem: analogue to the divine, nonetheless the act of writing involves him in forgery:

> The *Shin* then came to the fore and pleaded: O Lord of the world, may it please Thee to begin with me the world, seeing that I am the initial letter of thy name *ShaDDaI* (Almighty), and it is most fitting to create the world through that Holy Name. Said He in reply: Thou art worthy, thou art good, thou art true, but I may not begin through thee the creation of the world, since thou formest part of the group of letters expressing forgery, *ShekeR* (falsehood), which is not able to exist unless the *Koph* and *Resh* draw thee into their company. (Hence it is that a lie, to obtain credence, must always commence with something true. For the *shin* is a letter of truth, that letter by which the Patriarchs communed with God; but *koph* and *resh* are letters belonging to the evil side, which in order to stand firm attach to themselves the *shin.*[11]

It was here in the kabbalah that all of them might learn that in a word there was everything, and it was here, in fact, that Joyce and many of his contemporaries did learn that miracles of truth could be emergent from just such jocoserious juxtapositions as the Zoharic deity plays upon in the doubleness of *shin* the almighty forger. Ellmann gives us clues again to the psychobiography of Joyce the mystic in the role of Joyce the author: "Joyce not only binds fable to fact, but also fact to fable. He was forever trying to charm his life; his superstitions were attempts to impose sacramental importance upon naturalistic details. So too, his books were not to be taken as mere books, but as acts of prophecy. Joyce was capable of mocking his own claims of prophetic power . . . but he still made the claims."[12]

Let us take a small but significant instance. Joyce scoffed at the Theosophical Society, mocked clairvoyancy and its great mistress of fraud, Madame Blavatsky, in *Ulysses* ("O fie! . . . You oughtn't to look when a lady's a showing her elemental" [183]).

But when Lucia was in hospital Joyce wrote in circumstantial detail and pathetically excited tone to Harriet Weaver about a lost letter, the contents of which the girl had seemed to intuit. He prefaces the account with an affirmation as solemn as any Yeats ever offered: "Maybe I am an idiot but I attach the greatest importance to what Lucia says when she is talking about herself. Her intuitions are amazing. . . . My wife and I have seen hundreds of examples of her clairvoyance. Of course, I don't mean the juggling variety. But today we had a more than usually striking example" (*L,* I, 349: October 21, 1934).

This illustrates one serious version of the mystery of paternity which becomes the central exploration of *Ulysses*; indeed, the anecdote, taken together with all that we know of Joyce's obsession with his special access to Lucia, suggests the reaches of that "mystery" into natural orders incorporating and transcending any mythologies of fictional structure. Her breakdown came in 1932, and "the next seven years of Joyce's life were pervaded by a frantic and unhappily futile effort to cure her by every means known. . . . It seemed to him that her mind was like his own, and he tried to find evidence in her writing and in her drawing of unrecognized talent" (*L,* III, 7). "The poor child is just a poor girl who tried to do too much, to understand too much," Joyce wrote, "Her dependence on me is now absolute and all the affection she repressed for years pours itself out on both of us" (*L,* I, 346). Repeatedly, Joyce and Paul Leon write during Joyce's own major depression in 1933 of how affected her father has been in holding out hope for Lucia's improvement as the key to his own: "At present even when Miss Joyce is I think, decidedly better he comes across great difficulties and this improvement is entirely due to Mr. Joyce. And as regards himself though I repeat I find him much stronger he still perhaps as a reaction varies from states of great irritation and impotent fury to sudden lachrimose fits" (*L,* III, 275).

At one moment in the midst of frustrations, the "clairvoyancy" became as direct, strong, and inexplicably penetrating as any of the fictional moments of unlikely convergence between the psyches of Stephen and Bloom. The child prophesies in unwitting fashion the future of the father. Joyce writes to Giorgio in Italian of a conversation, prefacing it with this rhetorical remark: "Non so se credi alla chiaroveggenza" (I don't know if you believe in clairvoyance):

> Lucia: I was thinking all day about MacCormack. Why he was made a count instead of you. You are much greater. It is unfair. I was thinking I might write to the Pope. . . . But seriously, how long will the hostility between you and Ireland last? . . . I want to reconcile you: it is time that some influential Irishmen should come and shake hands with you after all you have done.
>
> Next morning at 7 the bellhop brought me a cable, the first and only message I have ever received from him, and the day after the *Irish Times* of Dublin published a long and rather favorable article on my last fragment, the first article which has appeared about me in the Irish press for twenty years. . . . apart from the prophecy, the very words are striking. She has sometimes the wisdom of the serpent and the innocence of the dove.[13]

We have been gathering some of Joyce's strange adventurings in paternity as it occupies a region between myth and mystery, between his names, his fictions, and himself. We can return now to the particular significance of Bloom's name in the penumbra of this context, recalling Shem the forger of the future. The explanation appears in the very opening section of the *Zohar,* and it institutes a prophecy of the prophecies that pass between fathers and children:

> In the beginning. R. Simeon opened his discourse with the text: *The blossoms appeared on the earth, etc.* (S. S. 2:12). . . . "The blossoms" [he said] are the patriarchs who pre-existed in the thought of the Almighty and later entered the world to come, where they were carefully preserved; from thence they issued secretly to become incarnate in the true prophets. . . . When do they become visible? . . . the time when the sinners are due to be cut off from the world; and they only escape because "the blossoms appear on the earth." . . . And who is it that upholds the world and causes the patriarchs to appear? It is the voice of tender children studying the Torah.[14]

Ulysses is a book of gradual revelation, a reading of the world of enigmatic symbols passed on from father to son, from the aging Jew to the visionary forger of a future art. It is a commentary opening the book of the world: "Signatures of all things

I am here to read, seaspawn and seawrack," says Stephen (*U*, 38). And it is in the seaspawn and seawrack, the great mother sea and the seashell that he is taught to read by Bloom, the patriarch chanting the Torah of his history in Hebraic phrases that touch responsive chords in the Stephen who hears at last "in a profound ancient male unfamiliar melody the accumulation of the past" (673). It is no accident that the teaching of the patriarchs is oral, and no coincidence that the kabbalah was once summed up as "the one voice among many voices of old Tradition which bears a message from the past to the modern world."[15]

II. *Forgery and Fraud: Creation and "Cosmic Consciousness"*

We must approach Joyce's own appropriation of the kabbalistic tradition by two avenues. First, there is the question of why this melange of early Jewish mystical texts would present itself as more than a curiosity or casual quarry. It is a question itself demanding a two-fold answer concerning the psychic appeal as well as the accessibility of these materials in Joyce's immediate environment. Second, there is the question of the nature of the kabbalah as it was available to Joyce in both its method and its symbolic contents.

We can perhaps best begin with Fiedler's observations on the narrow line dividing the "literary" child of nature in the nineteenth century and the charlatans and dupes of an esoteric subculture. Mantras and mystic cant, which form so large an element in our own recent "sub-culture," scarcely afflicted serious poetry outside of traveling academic roadshows by Allen Ginsberg, a bit of Bly, some formulas force-fed into the pastoral fantasies of Kerouac. But *vision* was a much more fluid word in the world that made fellows in a deep sense of Blavatsky, Mathers, and Yeats. It was still God's world, even as he seemed abandoning it. The yearning was as noble among the priests of aesthetic creation as it had been in that first Renaissance popularizer of kabbalistic secrets among the gentiles, Pico della Mirandola, who emulated the angelic mode of knowing deity. As priestly interpreters they could transmit the truth sometimes almost in the word as it had been spoken from on high. Little wonder that they felt a sense of fellowship in a community of the chosen with those who derived their own (often literal) inspiration from "elemental" messengers, voices apparently ready to illuminate the spiritual night by strange processes of synaesthesia in the imagination.

Let us insert a little irony, not irrelevant to the mood of meaningful coincidences in which Joyce moved. The Jewish kabbalah, as it was preserved in the *Zohar* is, indeed, an "ancient" text, emanating from the late Middle Ages. It is also a forgery presented as a document much more ancient than its literal birth; at once, then, scripture and fraud.

If Theophilus Gale had invited Ovid into his *Court of the Gentiles* while syncretizing Judaeo-Christian and classic mythologies for the seventeenth century and George Sandys simultaneously had invited inspired authors of the Pentateuch and the Gospels to fill his edition's margins with meanings for Ovid's *Metamorphoses* as "English'd" in those same decades, there were others then and later who grasped their relationship to the same syncretic tradition differently. Fraud: forgery. Both could be attempts to reassume contact with the past by participating in a single strain of spirituality which knows one voice in many without the *tuum* and *meum* of the more literal textual history. From the Cambridge Platonist Henry More's arrogant reconstruction of secret doctrines given to Moses on the Mount (the *Conjectura Cabbalistica* of 1653) to D'Annunzio's cry of triumph as a new and "truer" voice of Icarus is not a long imaginative leap. Nor are these "reconstructions" far removed from either extreme of the older mythic syncretism or modern fraud.

In the last years of the eighteenth century William Henry Ireland, inspired by his father's need for a contemporary Shakespeare, created one who incorporated Romantic pieties.[16] Almost in Joyce's birth year, Ireland's greater successor among Shakespeareans, J. Payne Collier, looked back from near the close of his long life with irony not untinged by triumph upon his interpolations into the hallowed texts: "If the emendations be forgeries how the inventor of them must laugh at the ridiculous result of his unrejectable fabrications: they now form an essential part of every new edition of Shakespeare, and never hereafter can be omitted."[17]

Collier's bitter smugness is not far removed in spirit from that of Stephen proving that Shakespeare "was not the father of his own son merely but, being no more a son, he was and felt himself the father of all his race, the father of his own grandfather" (*U,* 205). When Lyster and Best fall into collaboration with his theory, Stephen wryly admits he is faking it: "Both satisfied. I too. Don't tell them he was nine years old." But even as he extrapolates, Stephen "too" is satisfied with the theory of temporal lamination which makes all the spirit of the past a creation by the present: "What's in a name? That is what we ask ourselves in childhood when we write the name that we are told is ours" (207). And for Stephen, that name is again brought forward as that of his own mythic grandfather: "You make good use of the name, John Eglinton allowed. Your own name is strange enough." "Fabulous artificer," thinks Stephen, "the hawklike man" (206).

If biographical forgeries in the spirit of the time were a temptation offered Stephen by past successes, they raised no less an issue than the relation between genius and the past. Genius could, and many of Joyce's models and contemporaries believed it should invent its own aesthetic heritage; "invent" in the double sense of the word's root as discovery and creation. It is instructive that in Trieste young Joyce owned the Ossian poems of James MacPherson in English, German, and Italian.[18] Blake could scold Wordsworth's quiet scepticism with: "I Believe both MacPherson & Chatterton, that what they say is Ancient Is so. I own myself an admirer of Ossian equally with any other Poet whatever, Rowley & Chatterton also."[19] Byron had to adopt a more sophisticated and daring attitude, which carried over into Joyce's own time and temperament: "I fear Laing's late edition has completely overthrown every hope that MacPherson's Ossian might prove the translation of a series of poems complete in themselves; but while the imposture is discovered, the merit of the work remains undisputed." Hazlitt classed Ossian with Dante, Homer, and the

Bible,[20] and in Joyce's own time Alfred Nutt, accepting the "imposture," cast it aside as irrelevant to that brilliance which placed MacPherson beside yet another honored peer: "He undoubtedly had some knowledge of the Ossianic ballad literature existing in the highlands in his day, and he worked up many of its themes into his English Ossian, which is, however, almost as much his own composition as 'Paradise Lost' is the composition of Milton. He suffered himself to maintain the existence of a Gaelic original. . . . But MacPherson's flashes of genuine inspiration . . . will always secure for him a high place."[21]

The debate over the authenticity of the old monk Thomas Rowley was long laid when David Masson wrote in 1899 of the wondrous boy Thomas Chatterton:

> These Antique Poems . . . are perhaps as worthy of being still read as many portions of the poetry of Byron, Shelley, or Keats. . . . Chatterton's archaisms, . . . pseudo-archaisms though they were, belonged to his very mood when he wrote the poems, and swayed his imagination in the production of them; they are essential, therefore, . . . and no editor has a right to tamper with them any more than . . . with that artificial archaism of Spenser's language which was part of *his* device for distancing himself from the world of the present, and carrying his readers back with him into an imaginary world of the Arthurian past.[22]

Just before young Joyce left Paris in the early spring of 1903 that city saw the culmination of a notorious art fraud that had begun in 1896 when a Russian merchant appeared in Vienna with a number of ancient artifacts, including the sumptuous golden tiara of Saitaphernes dating from the third century B.C. The president of the French Republic urged its acquisition by the Louvre, a purchase engineered and defended by the directors and a committee. Immediately questions of authenticity were raised around the Homeric reliefs encircling the piece, creating a stir in the Paris press which was, nonetheless, resolved in favor of the champions of the ancients in 1899. All would perhaps have rested there had not another charge of forged drawings been exploited by *Le Matin* of Paris in the spring of 1903. Salomon Reinach, spokesman for the original purchase committee, publicly asked: "Where could one find the forger of such a masterpiece? Where is this exceptional individual?" The exceptional individual was a Russian goldsmith named Ruchomowsky. He arrived in Paris a week before Joyce left the city for Dublin and *Dubliners.* To the newspapers Ruchomowsky boasted of genius's triumph over time as boldly as any artificer of myths: "The tiara is no work of art, it is crude work. You should see my sarcophagus." The sarcophagus was at that moment being exhibited in the Salon des artistes de France in a show of ancient art.[23]

Sharing Paris with Joyce and Ruchomowsky during this spring was another forger whose work would later shape important aspects of *Ulysses.* He was S. L. MacGregor Mathers, in 1903 engaged in violent feud with William Butler Yeats. The arena was the Order of the Golden Dawn, originated by Mathers and William Wynn Westcott in London in the late 1880s on the basis of forged authorization from the German Rosicrucian "Soror Sapiens Dominabitur Astris" (nee Sprengel). Mathers's own authority stemmed not only from his fraudulent titles (Comte de Glenstrae or Comte MacGregor) and his pretensions to esoteric access to Rosicrucian traditions, the Tarot, and other magic, but also from his translation of parts of Knorr von Rosenroth's *Kabbala Denudata,* a seventeenth-century Latin version of the Jewish kabbalah. Mathers's version had been published in 1887 as *The Kabbalah Unveiled.* That authority had been undermined through a myriad of comic internecine quarrels within the Isis-Urania Temple of the Golden Dawn in London during Mathers's self-exile to Paris, and during 1902 and 1903 Yeats had assumed irenic administrative authority.[24]

My "initiation into the 'Hermetic Students' had filled my head with Cabbalistic imagery," Yeats reports in *A Vision,*[25] adding that "'Michael Robartes' had founded a society . . . for the study of [Rosenroth's] *Kabbala Denudata* and similar books."[26] This is late, but in *The Celtic Twilight* of 1893 Yeats had already written passages later self-annotated with the observation that "MacGregor Mathers and his pupils" taught him "to so suspend the will that the imagination moved of itself."[27]

In 1901 Yeats was willing to do battle with Mathers in the

interest of preserving the Golden Dawn and, paradoxically, preserving its allegiance to Mathers's own call upon an authority based in "magic." However, whereas Mathers had claimed a hieratic authority based in ritual magic culminating in private access to astral powers, Yeats believed in the magic of the imagination's access to the past and its poetic voice. Within the parochial context of the Order, Yeats in that year wrote a *religio* in the affirmative on the question "Is the Order of R.R. & A.C. to remain a Magical Order?"[28] More publicly he wrote the essay "Magic" which, in George Harper's phrase, "is clearly intended as a kind of credo of the Romantic artist."[29] The description seems too broad and too narrow; "Magic" is a rationale for the pretensions of the mystic-mythic artist which is more descriptive of *Ulysses* and *Finnegans Wake* than of *A Vision.*

At base, Yeats's essay is a practical illustration of that power of one imagination over another which seemed to lay behind that special "clairvoyance" which so marvelously connected the psyches of Joyce and his daughter Lucia. But as instances multiply in Yeats's experience he comes to realize that the magical connections are evoked by symbols shared through the ages, waiting with all their dormant history in an akasic state similar to that described by that other contemporary mystic, A. P. Sinnett, and transferred by Joyce into the "Aeolus" chapter.[30] It is less that our participation in the great memory offers perennial symbols, however, than that the powers of symbols "act . . . because the great memory associates them with certain events and moods and persons. Whatever the passions of man have gathered about, becomes a symbol in the great memory, and in the hands of him who has the secret, it is a worker of wonders."[31] Indeed, this passage explains two of the "three doctrines" Yeats sets forth at the beginning: "That the borders of our memories are . . . shifting, and that our memories are a part of one great memory," and "That this great mind and great memory can be evoked by symbols" (21). Joyce's milieu was saturated with the experience of this access; within months D'Annunzio would describe his own succession to the imagination and role of Icarus during composition of the mythic dithyramb: "It was not he who yearned in me, not he who cried out in me; but rather I cried out in him . . . I battered myself like an ardent eagle in a blind cage."

The third Yeatsian "doctrine" is perhaps the most interesting, in being explicit about that imaginative epistemology claimed alike by poet, prophet, forger, and fraud: "That the borders of our mind are ever shifting, and that many minds can flow into one another, as it were, and create or reveal a single mind, a single energy" (21). Chatterton and young Ireland had probably half-believed something very similar, and the mythical historian D'Annunzio would have grappled the notion to his several poetic bosoms. Joyce, creator of those multiple personae whose substitution for the author simultaneously encase him in and exclude him from the work, would appreciate Yeats's version of shifting minds as narratorial technique. At the house of a magus, Yeats has heard a rather allegorical, yet indeterminate gothic vision-tale revelatory of some past existence of his own. "It had not," he says, "the personal significance of the other vision, but was certainly strange and beautiful. . . . Who was it made the story, if it were but a story? I did not, and the seeress did not, and the evoker of spirits did not and could not. It arose in three minds. . . . One mind was doubtless the master, I thought, but all the minds gave a little, creating for a moment what I must call a supernatural artist" (30–31).

This shared evocation that becomes a narratorless narrative, however, can be looked at in a way that gives resonance to Leslie Fiedler's observation about becoming a child of nature in the nineteenth century: "One becomes, in so far as he fails, a *literary* version of the child of nature; and, in so far as he succeeds, a creature of subculture: of the world of 'cosmic consciousness.'"[32] One can, that is, see the creative activity of the magical imagination in such a way as to explain Chatterton's or MacPherson's pseudo-primitivism as a distorted employment of a sound vision. And one can see, too, how these forgeries were genuine adumbrations of the mystic mythologies of Joyce's Homeric kabbalah, how each could potentially become what Yeats called "magic." "Barbaric people," Yeats argues, receive the symbolic influences of the great memory, the akasic bank of human passions, "more visibly and obviously, and in all likelihood more easily and fully than we do, for our life in cities, which deafens or kills the meditative life," has desensitized us (36–37). But the ultimate aim of Victorian poet and vatic enchanter is one—to bridge in himself otherness in past and present until they merge at the heart of the great mind's symbolic memory:

> Men who are imaginative writers today may well have preferred to influence the imagination of others more directly in past times. Instead of learning their craft with paper and a pen they may have sat for hours imagining themselves to be stocks and stones and beasts of the wood till the images were so vivid that the passers-by became but a part of the imagination of the dreamer, and wept or laughed or ran away as he would have them. Have not poetry and music arisen, as it seems out of the sounds the enchanters made to help their imagination to enchant. . . . at whatever risk, we must cry out that imagination is always seeking to remake the world according to the impulses and the patterns in that great Mind, and that great Memory. . . . speaking of what has been, and shall be again, in the consummation of time.
>
> (39, 49)

III. *Modern Mystagogues and Ancient Texts: The Kabbalah Again Revived*

So much could Yeats take for poetry from the fraud and forgery of MacGregor Mathers, even while wresting from him the leadership of the Golden Dawn. Simultaneously, Arthur Edward Waite had added to the fallen master's indignities in a series of schemes by which he had taken physical possession of the elaborately painted ritual vault of the London Temple from Mathers's allies in spite of Aleister Crowley's attempted invasion on Mathers's behalf "in Highland dress, a black mask over his face, . . . an enormous gold or gilt cross on his breast, and a dagger at his side."[33] Waite, the most dazzling combination of scholar and mystic of the early twentieth century, would devastatingly trace the fictitious genealogy of Mathers's Golden Dawn[34] and repeatedly rend his *Kabbalah Unveiled* as an uncritical, uninformed, and secondhand translation.[35] But this did not prevent him from acknowledging enthusiastically, "There has been always . . . a certain class of students for whom the claims made by and on behalf of the Kabbalah have possessed importance, and this class is possibly larger now than at any time prior to the date of 1865."[36]

It is the burden of this chapter to demonstrate that Joyce was of this class, and that the kabbalistic translations and commentaries of those two antagonists on the field of Jewish esoterica who were so intimately involved with Yeats were no less crucial in the conception and construction of *Ulysses*. The argument will seem surprising to some constant readers of Joyce, but should not.

It is true that Stephen Dedalus mocks contemporary mysticism in the person of Madame Blavatsky and in her influence upon Dubliners in the "National Library" chapter of *Ulysses*, and we have accounts of a drunken raid with Gogarty upon the chambers of the Dublin Hermetic Society.[37] It is relevant to recall, though, that he also derides the "hellenizing" ambitions of Mulligan in spite of the title and the Homeric parallel. That did not prevent his younger avatar from being both a modern Irishman and a mythic Greek. Nor did an informed scepticism about the excesses of Dublin theosophy and hermeticism prevent Joyce from making Bloom the only Jewish protagonist in English literature since Milton's epics. That his name, too, was drawn from a mythology has been suggested already: Hellenic and Hebraic mythologies syncretizing through the interplay of a son from the one and a father from the other.

Waite was right in observing the contemporary influence of the Jewish kabbalah. Sinnett and others had prepared the way with the wave of theosophic syncretism at best and medium communication at worst which, with shifting and overlapping personnel, connected the adepts, scholars, poets, and frauds of Dublin, London, and Paris for the better part of four decades from the 1880s through the publication of *Ulysses*.[38] But the kabbalah proper became an ancient hidden doctrine paradoxically universalized into European mysticism and theology at just this time through MacGregor Mathers's selective translations from the *Zohar* in *The Kabbalah Unveiled* (1887) and Waite's two learned interpretations,

The Doctrine and Literature of the Kabalah (1902) and *The Secret Doctrine in Israel* (1913), the latter appearing just as Joyce was beginning to shape *Ulysses.* Simultaneously with Waite's interpretations, the first major translation of the *Zohar* into the modern vernacular was being published in Paris when Emile LaFamu-Giraud of the Asiatic Society of France posthumously edited Jean de Pauly's *Sepher Ha-Zohar (Le Livre de la Splendeur)* in six volumes appearing between 1906 and 1911. Joyce undoubtedly turned to the latter in the course of his weaving of *Ulysses,* as he must have done with von Rosenroth's original. But it was the books by Mathers and Waite which provided the symbolic underpinning holding *Ulysses* together as a mystic rather than merely mythic text written out of those years when for so many minds the border between the two modes of thought were excitingly indiscernible.[39]

So much for the question of the accessibility of the kabbalah for Joyce. Now let us turn to the second question posed concerning the nature of this strange and popular book as it offered itself not only as quarry but, in ways as obvious as unexpected, a model for the "new" narrative mode of *Ulysses.* To do so is to remind ourselves once more that Joyce's narrative is fulfilled—completed, if one will—beyond the realization of the characters, and that the old debate about the primacy of surface or symbol creates a false dichotomy. What A. E. Waite offered as preparative instruction for reading the *Zohar* is eminently useful as prolegomenon to *Ulysses:* "It is only as if casually that the word interpretation can be held to apply in any solid sense; the Secret Doctrine is rather the sense below the sense which is found in the literal word—as if one story were written on the obverse side of the parchment and another on the reverse side."[40]

Ulysses, like the *Zohar,* offers events that are interpreted symbolically only because of the juxtaposition of another symbolic system that paradoxically results in exegesis of the surface action while maintaining its own integrity at a completely arbitrary distance. That is, we have no allegorizing or emblematic tendency directing the commentary within the text upon the action of the protagonists. That action serves, rather, to trigger a large surrounding world of meanings in which it ultimately takes its limited historical place, a place at once larger and smaller than the allegorical heroics and ironies of the perspective from which the Homeric parallels force us, to use an instance documented by Joyce himself, into evaluating Bloom as a new Ulyssean everyman.

I have suggested above, in citing the paternal blooms with which the *Zohar* opens, and will detail below how its symbols were employed by Joyce. And I have emphasized that the method of interaction between scriptural text and kabbalistic "interpretation" was adapted as his own in his making of *Ulysses.* These are highly meaningful, central elements; but it is sometimes the trivial or, at best, meaninglessly literal adaptation that most clearly reveals the enthusiast's debt (and certainly Joyce the mythographer, mythologist, proto-mystic, was, for all the sceptical posing, an enthusiast). Let us then recognize how initially improbable seem Joyce's elaborate and jealously guarded charts for colors, organs, and such governing each chapter of *Ulysses.*[41] They have done less for interpreters, offered fewer guides to image clusters, than some of Joyce's more casual comments. Few pre-Joycean works have been so schematized, certainly not the *Odyssey,* and certainly no work so strikingly as the *Zohar,* with its progressively self-complicating charts of the relations among the *sephiroth* and their symbolic counterparts. For both books are systems at once abstract and concrete, "myriad metamorphoses of symbol," in Joyce's phrase, in which the abstractions are sometimes mirrored in, but always attached to, the most trivial details of physical reality: a world of colors, in which (to use the kabalistic terms as translated by Mathers for Joyce's Dublin) primordial Microprosopus reflects physically the abstract nature of projected Macroprosopus.[42] The mode of conception is immediately apparent when one thumbs the schemata plates in Mathers's *Kabbalah Unveiled* and then turns to learn that kidneys are related to economics and orange, while the esophagus is in special kinship with architecture within the Joycean cosmos. Reduced to the absurd, the "Greater Holy Assembly" (Ha Idra Zuta Rabba Quadisha) and the "Lesser Holy Assembly" (Ha Idra Zuta

Quadisha) which make up the largest part of Mathers's translations present themselves as studies in correspondencies which concentrate not only upon organs but upon the meaning of the several hairs of Macroprosopus' beard. I am suggesting that Joyce was so drawn into the world of kabbalism as a structure that could be transmuted into a new fictional form that he followed the curve of the kabbalistic psyche even when it led into private and fruitless deserts, "secret" doctrine, indeed, in Madame Blavatsky's sense. But the returns for *Ulysses* were well worth the small losses, and it is to the impact of that kabbalistic world upon the making and meaning of *Ulysses* that we should now turn.

IV. Ulysses: *Joyce's Kabbalah*

> They (the vague mystical yearnings of man) can . . . fitly be compared to that invisible chain that binds husband to wife, parents to children. . . . Without these lesser mysticisms society would dissolve into its first atoms.
>
> Harry Sperling, in *Aspects of the Hebrew Genius*

I

The narrative in *Ulysses* is so ambiguous that it has from the start invited a simple division of critical view, no matter how sophisticated the defences flung up on either side may become. The book is about a return home, about two wanderers seeking communication, about Ulysses and Telemachus and Penelope. The wanderers come together in the household of Penelope, they talk, they part. Communication, communion, atonement, has occurred or it has not. Bloom will awaken in the morning to receive breakfast in bed, Stephen will be reconciled with history as humaneness—or all will go on as it has been, the protagonists brushing aside the tired night encounter with its timid gestures of release and false intimations of hope. It is within the matrix of this search for connection that all interpretations of whatever persuasion must be born and from which they must take direction.

Let us look first at the negative evidence. Early in 1893 Molly Bloom one morning looked out of the window of her Raymond Terrace apartment to see two dogs copulating in the street. As a grinning police sergeant who saw her must have realized, the sight excited the young wife, who begged her husband: "Give us a touch, Poldy. God, I'm dying for it" (*U,* 88). That, Bloom meditates on June 16, 1904, is "How life begins." But the result of this animal-inspired copulation was a very brief life, that of Rudy Bloom, male heir to the young couple, who will in the phantasmagoric night of Bloomsday arise as a vision fused with the fallen Stephen Dedalus whom Bloom protects and paternally attempts to adopt. In anticipation of Rudy's birth, Leopold and Molly suspended sexual relations on November 27, 1893. The child was born on December 29, but died eleven days later (Mrs. Thornton, the midwife, "knew from the first poor little Rudy wouldn't live" [66]). It was at this traumatic moment that all sexual intercourse between them was finished, in spite of Molly's recognition that Bloom "understood or felt what a woman is" (767), in spite of his being virile and poetically exciting enough to make her lose her breath as he took her on the hill of Howth on September 10, 1888 (767), conceiving their first child and necessitating marriage a month later. As the scientific cataloguer of the "Ithaca" chapter notes, "there remained a period of 10 years, 5 months and 18 days during which carnal intercourse has been incomplete" (721). Worse, the negative prospect for any renewal of intercourse seems absolute: "The parties, if now disunited were obliged to reunite for increase and multiplication, which was absurd, to form by reunion the original couple of uniting parties, which was impossible" (711). Worse yet, since from Milly's first menstrual period on "15 September 1903, there remained a period of 9 months and 1 day" during which complete mental intercourse between himself [Bloom] and the listener [Molly] had not taken place . . . in consequence of a preestablished natural comprehension in incomprehension between the consummated females" (721). Bloom feels victimized by his wife and daughter's redoubled checks upon his movements as Milly intuits Molly's jealous suspicions ("complete corporal liberty of action had been circumscribed. . . . By various reiterated feminine interrogation"); Molly feels circumscribed, her frustration heightened, by Milly's new sexual curiosity ("I couldn't turn round with her in the place lately unless I bolted the door first . . . coming in without knocking first when I put the chair against the door just as I was washing myself there below with the glove" [751]). The consequence of all this has been Molly's flagrant adultery and Bloom's crippled fantasy that leads him to masturbate to the ironic observation that every bullet finds its billet.

Yet the irony may be more superficial than this history would suggest. June 16 has been a day of intense self-observation and decision-making on the part of both Bloom and Molly, and he is billetted with her, at home. At the close of the night, a different day already dawning, Bloom crawls into bed in a position of inverted symmetry with Molly, head to tail, once more not sexually successful, but at rest together, complements completing a movement in the form of a renewed whole: "the childman weary, the manchild in the womb. Womb? Weary? He rests. He has travelled" (*U,* 722).

II

Sex is, Waite emphatically repeats in many portions of his work, the central mystery of the kabbalah.[43] And at the beginning of a chapter of *The Secret Doctrine in Israel* titled "The Mystery of Sex" he explains: "It follows that he who, in Zoharic terminology, suffers his fount to fail and produces no fruits here—whether because he will not take a wife, whether his wife is barren, or whether he abides with her in a way that is against Nature—commits an irreparable crime."[44] Leopold Bloom certainly abides with Molly in a way that is against nature, but their inverted bed position is a consequence, not cause of the abortive birth of Rudy. How, then, if we are to test the presence of a kabbalistic sub- or supra-text, has this sinful barrenness been brought upon the once-fertile Blooms?

The first mistake was to conceive little Rudy on that morning long ago, since "nuptial intercourse is interdicted during the day," explains Waite, owing to the kabbalistic interpretation of Genesis 27:11.[45] This, though, was merely literal defiance of the law, and a deeper spiritual lapse was the conception of the child because Molly's fantasy had been stimulated by her view of the dogs' copulation. We have been aware of Stephen's antipathy to dogs, and the perennial blasphemous potential of inverting God and dog (the *Finnegans Wake* version is "dog in a manger") which feeds into Mulligan's "dogsbody" (*U*, 7). The inversion by Molly and Bloom becomes a link in this tradition, if one pursues the kabbalistic teachings on the mysteries of sex. Stephen recognizes in the dog, dead or destructive, that animal of death he recognizes also in the black panther of his dream; the Blooms embrace the vision of the dogs, incorporating their animalistic mating as a life stimulus. But the kabbalistic injunction against barrenness is predicated upon the holy sexual communion, not only between man and woman ("soul as well as body shares in the *gaudium inexprimabile* by which children are engendered"[46]), but between man and god:

> . . . there is also a consequence within the measures of the union itself so that it is raised from the physical into the spiritual degree, from the mode of Nature into the mode of grace. The fulfillment of a particular precept is the condition attaching thereto and this is the raising of the heart and mind, on the part of the Lover and Beloved, to the most Holy Shekinah, the glory which cohabits and indwells, during the external act. . . . Out of this arises the question as to when man may be called one, and . . . this comes about when the male is united to the female in a holy purpose. . . . It is of this that the man and the woman must think at the moment of their union . . . in uniting bodies and souls . . . [the man] draws down the Holy Spirit upon him and is called Son of the Holy One.[47]

Bloom's mistake in his tragic mediated imitation of the dogs rather than his God is, one supposes, the symbolic stimulus for the narrative incident in which the citizen's Garryowen mauls at him. And, more than Nora Barnacle's miscarriage,[48] this must account for the infant death of Rudy which frustrated Bloom's Hebraic hope of paternity and led to the Blooms' renunciation of sexual intercourse.

One result of this abstention among the events of Bloomsday ("for the Hebrews include all this time of their exile in the space of one day"[49]) is the "rite of Onan" (*U,* 713) enjoyed by Bloom as he watches Gerty McDowell with erotic fantasy in full play. This masturbation is a compounding of the original sin, venial at the surface level of the plot but terrible in its kabbalistic context. The spilling of blood which led to the flood is interpreted in the *Zohar* as the spilling of man's seed.[50] Waite explained, "The sex aberration here designated will be understood by the expression used. It is the crime attributed to Onan, and the Zoharic doctrine affirms that no man who is sullied in this manner shall enter the heavenly palace nor behold the face of Sekinah."[51]

Bloom, then, is doubly removed from his entrance into union with the Holy One by his corrupt sexual practices with both Molly and himself. And so he has become a father without a son, a husband without a wife, a patriarch without a god. And yet the Blooms are the patriarchs and true prophets. And the archetype is that ubiquitous visitor to *Ulysses,* Moses: "from Moses . . . to Moses . . . there arose none like Moses" (*U,* 671).[52]

Moses himself, the kabbalistic tradition taught, had a limitation like Bloom's. We know that, unable to enter the promised land, he had only a Pisgah sight of Palestine, a myth used by Stephen in one direction and zoharic commentators in another. The kabbalah transmuted Moses' abortive journey into a sexual symbolism to be read doubly: spiritually as effect but physically as cause:

> Now, there is an appendix to the *Sepher Yetzirah* concerning 50 Gates of Understanding . . . this ascription is countenanced by the Zohar when it is said that these Gates are in the region of the Supreme Mother, who gives power to the Mother below—a reference to the Shekinah in transcendence and in manifestation. . . . The 50 Gates are another symbolism concerning the . . . journey through the great distance, for the first gate is in matter and the last is in God Himself; but this gate was not . . . opened by Moses—because . . . he ceased to cohabit with his wife on earth.[53]

At the close of *Ulysses* Bloom the patriarch,[54] like Moses the patriarch, cannot enter the last gate of wisdom, possession of a full union of consciousness or carnality with Molly. The failure is foreshadowed by his lacking the entrance key to 7 Eccles Street upon his return, a failure that again leads back to the psychophysical symbols of the *Zohar*. MacGregor Mathers explains, with the aid of some parenthetic footnotes, that

> . . . the mother is illuminated (that is, in the second part of the ordinary averse Tetragrammaton, which consists of the letters IH. . . . and is opened out into her gates (that is, if these two letters be bound closely together then . . . the pentad originateth the number 50, by which are denoted the fifty gates of the understanding). . . . The key is added which containeth sex, and closeth its gate. (That is, in the third part of this averse form, which is IHV.) . . .[55]

Bloom, like Moses, has lost his key and his wife—yet like *Moses* he has lost them. Moses was the great teacher of his people, and the *Zohar* is largely a commentary upon the history he taught in the Pentateuch, as Bloom is the patriarch who flowers briefly in the night to teach the Torah to another child questing in history for a voice that may not be that of God, but that will lead from the cacophony of "a shout in the street" to the comfort of "a profound ancient male unfamiliar melody."

The separation of Leopold and Molly Bloom is one of the moot ambivalences upon which so many commentaries have broken by making a simpler choice than the novel authorizes. To this point we have consulted only the negative evidence, the sexual alienation, the adultery, even the loss of "complete mental intercourse." Yet Molly's first word is a "*no*" addressed to Bloom in the morning, and her last a "*yes*" of union as Bloom sleeps at her side and she relives in memory her first surrender to him "lying among the rhododendrons on Howth head" when "he said I was a flower of the mountain yes so we are flowers . . . yes that was why I liked him because I saw he understood or felt what a woman is" (*U,* 767). She has finally activated her adulterous fancies ("well its done now once and for all with all the talk of the world about it people make its only the first time after that its just ordinary" [725]), and in the aftermath of her adventure with the enormous "Stallion" Boylan, she knows that "Poldy has more spunk in him" (727), is still jealous of Josie Powell after all of the years, and proud of her own achievement in marrying the superior Bloom—at once knowledgeable and considerate.[56] Bloom, of course, seldom has Molly from his thoughts in the course of the day, from his opening offer to serve breakfast in bed to his final request to be served breakfast in bed. He shares her jealousy and shares her connubial pride, both coloring his numerous accounts of the forthcoming concert tour. And at the close, as earlier remarked, they lie together united in antisexual symmetry, in a union beyond sexuality: "the childman weary, the manchild in the womb. . . . He rests. He has travelled" (722). All the creative "Sephiroth will be in a certain degree androgynous," Mathers explained,[57] and the same is true of their totality, the expression of the Holy One, Shekinah.

> The Shekinah is the Liberating Angel who delivers the world in all ages. . . . But it is stated that this Liberating Angel manifests as male and female, being male when it dispenses the celestial benedictions on the world below . . . but when charged with offices of judgement it is called female, as a woman who carries her child in the womb . . . the interchange of sex in divine things must be understood throughout. . . . Now, it is said that Shekinah is to Metatron [the angelic creative principle] what the Sabbath is to the weekdays . . . she is rest, and the rapture of rest, yet it is that rest in which there is the intercourse of spiritual union.[58]

In Joyce's Irish kabbalah the mystery of sex reconciles the apparent conflict of interpretation. In animal lust Bloom forsook the blessings of creativity. The cost was to cast out the Jew forever to wander without a key to the last gate, which lay in Molly's loins. He can have no child, not even a Stephen, and in this sense suffers the Mosaic punishment that the kabbalah and the human psyche place upon all of those who fail to see both surface *and* symbol in the act of love. Yet, too, he returns home to rest in Molly's physical warmth, psychic empathy, and symbolic womb—"that rest in which there is the intercourse of spiritual union."

III

He rests. But "he has travelled." Ulysses, of course, was a traveler, but Bloom sets out to none of the big wars that make ambition virtue, only to his daily routine business as ad canvasser. It is in the newspaper office that this interest in business affairs is most prominent, and here, too, that Moses dominates the conversation. Let us observe a typically Joycean indirection. As some newsprint-oriented modern narrator has been interspersing commentary upon each stage of the conversation by means of headlines in this chapter, so Stephen had been allusively and stylistically satirizing the same conversation within his own consciousness. While Bloom telephones and the others begin to leave, "Messenger took out his match-box thoughtfully and lit his cigar" (*U,* 138). The "messenger" is J. J. O'Molloy, who is preparing to recite "one of the most polished periods I think I ever listened to in my life [which] fell from the lips of Seymour Bushe" (137). Bushe's rhetoric concerns Michelangelo's Moses, "that stony effigy in frozen music, horned and terrible, of the human form divine, that eternal symbol of wisdom and prophecy" (138). Between the lighting of the cigar and the memorial recitation Stephen interjects a private tongue-in-cheek commentary that cannot refer to the irrelevant O'Molloy: "I have often thought since on looking back over that strange time that it was that small act, trivial in itself, that striking of that match, that determined the whole aftercourse of our lives" (138). A joke about fictional styles, but one begging for interpretation, since the pause allows Bloom to catch Myles Crawford and be rejected, but a Bloom, whose analogue is Moses and whose future duty is to inform Stephen. Like Moses, Bloom is a prophet and a teacher; but like Bloom, the teachers of the kabbalistic tradition are travelers in the world who carry the knowledge of their separation and their union with them as a portable wisdom:

> The principle is that the male must be always attached to the female for the Shekinah ever to be with him . . . those who had the precept at heart and were therefore complete men by their union with women on earth . . . were travellers in search of wisdom; and they were also men of affairs, workers in the vineyard of the world. . . . The Zohar is full of their little journeys . . . strange people went about in those days carrying, unknown to one another, the treasures of mystic knowledge. . . . Now, journeys in search of wisdom or in the prosecution

> of business—which, it may be mentioned, was often of a humble kind—meant separation from the wife . . . and this would seem at first sight to involve separation from Shekinah. To remove this difficulty it was held sufficient [that the traveler should guard his actions as though the Shekinah were present] . . . it postulates the dwelling of Shekinah with man. The word cohabiting seems to be an incorrect word, for it was obviously in an inward sense only that the Shekinah accompanied the Sons of the Doctrine in their recurring voyages and ventures . . . they seem to have been conscious of a certain marriage state—spiritually realized—in their relation with her.[59]

Bloom is the Mosaic traveling teacher, united with and separated from Molly, whose apparently humble duty is to place an ad in the world of print, but whose shadow passes Stephen here long before their brush at the door of the National Library, the shadow of a patriarch bearing the treasures of mystic knowledge.

IV

Most of this discussion has been directed to the closing portions of *Ulysses,* where the convergence of Bloom, Molly, and Stephen is culminated. From the patriarchal/paternal associations of Bloom's name through his marital and sexual difficulties, our course and that of *Ulysses* has followed the curve of what we might call the symbolic narrative of kabbalistic travel.

However, for all the emphasis that Waite and others put upon sex as the informing force of the *Zohar,* within its massive analysis of correspondences certain other symbols emerge so frequently as to dominate its strange semimetaphysical litany. They are the sea, the shell, the ear, and the voice. And to realize their immense impact upon Joyce's novel we should now turn back to the beginning, where these symbols are implanted into *Ulysses* (along with Joyce's allusion to their kabbalistic source), and work toward the middle, where their consequences for the conclusion are elaborately worked out for Bloom's consciousness in "Sirens." It is here that Bloom demonstrates his Ulyssean shrewdness about human character, about the character of woman. After a day of avoidance, he sights Blazes Boylan almost at the hour of the assignation with Molly. Suddenly determined, he follows him to the Ormond bar, weighs the consequences of frustrating the adultery, and decides to let it proceed to its natural end. Wise, but anxiously reluctant, he sits with Richie Goulding listening to Simon Dedalus sing as Boylan leaves the bar. Nostalgia sets in for those days when both Dedalus and the Blooms had been happier in midst of the musical society of Dublin: "The nights Si sang. The human voice, two tiny silky cords. Wonderful, more than all the others" (*U,* 272).

Hours earlier on Sandymount Strand the image had been Stephen's, tying him into the nightmare of history, a strangling, consubstantial umbilical: "The cords all link back, strandentwining cable of all flesh" (*U,* 39). Here in "Proteus," come "to read, seaspawn and seawrack," Stephen's "boots crush crackling wrack and shells" (38). We are reminded that in "Nestor" Stephen's associational pattern had identified shells with a collection of Stuart coins kept by Deasy and thence with the deathmask in which history seems to confront the young teacher: "Stephen's embarrassed hand moved over the shells heaped in the cold stone mortar . . . dead treasure, hollow shells" (30). This nightmare sense of a dead past haunts Stephen's walk along the beach: the poor mariners appear as "Human shells" (42), a drowned man is recollected as swept along with "silly shells" (50), Stephen's rotting teeth are mere "Shells" (51). It is in this context that Stephen envisions history as a throttling universal umbilical and articulates his desire to cut it, to remain outside the historical network. And it is the moment at which Joyce offers his explicit notice of a kabbalistic element in *Ulysses,* as Stephen jocoseriously imagines a cosmic phone call: "The cords of all link back . . . cable of all flesh. . . . Will you be as gods? Gaze in your omphalos. Hello. . . . Put me on to Edenville. Aleph, alpha: nought, nought one. Spouse and helpmate of Adam Kadmon: Heva, naked Eve. She had no navel" (39). *Adam Kadmon* is the *Zohar's* image of the supernal world expressed as man, even as Adam will be expressed in the image of that supernal world: as Waite succinctly puts it, "this world is regarded as the abode of *Adam Kadmon,* who is also its sole denizen."[60] This version fuses with the joke about the call, incorporating allusion to the numerical values of the Hebrew alphabet into Stephen's fearful pride in wanting to be "as a god."

The *Zohar* relates that when the Holy One "came to create the world, all the letters presented themselves before him" in reverse order to press their claims. All were rejected (we have seen the example of *shin* above) until *beth* stood forth and God said: "Assuredly, with thee I will create the world, and thou shalt form the beginning in the creation of the world." *Aleph* stood quietly by until the lord turned and teased her obvious disappointment before explaining: "Aleph, Aleph, although I will begin the creation of the world with the *beth* . . . my unity shall not be expressed except through thee."[61] The telephonic umbilical cords identify Stephen's nightmare as inverted dream, the ultimate dream of the primitivist: he would escape the endlessly bifurcated historical world of *beth* and enter not only into apotheosis, but into the uncreative unity of *aleph.* But this he envisions as retreat into the mythic paradise of Eve without a navel, the Urmother's undifferentiating womb. Stephen as existential coward would steal that rest that Bloom the traveling patriarchal teacher will earn when he at last rests with Molly, "the manchild in the womb." Mulligan, of course, had hailed the sea as the "great sweet mother" (*U,* 7) and this association leads Stephen to define his dilemma in metaphoric narrative.[62] Mulligan has recently rescued a man from drowning, and Stephen questions his own fears in contrast: "I would want to. I would try. I am not a strong swimmer. . . . Do you see the tide flowing quickly in on all sides, sheeting the lows of sand quickly, shell-cocoacoloured? If I had land under my feet. I want his life still to be his, mine to be mine" (45–46).

Stephen's dilemma is insoluble. Wanting the private ahistoricity of the unbifurcated paradise, a world static from everlasting to everlasting, he still finds that he must shuffle on the shells of that history (seawrack) which threatens him with limitation, with a heritage at one end and death at the other. He would want to save the drowning man if he could do it without commitment, each retaining his separate identity untouched. It is the Stephen who meets his sister Dilly at the bookstall, recognizes her need, his own, and retreats into the image of his mother's death which he has carried from the first pages of *Ulysses:* "She is drowning. Agenbite. Save her. . . . She will drown me with her, eyes and hair. Lank coils of seaweed hair around me, my heart, my soul. Salt green death" (*U,* 240).

It is worth recalling the mythic paradoxes in *A Portrait* upon which we closed the discussion of the previous chapter. When we do so, it is as if Stephen has retained the hydrophobic fears of Icarus and forgotten the aesthetic and, in the widest sense, paternal ambitions of Daedalus, forgotten the laminations of Irish muse which unite the Blessed Virgin, the dark peasant, and the bird-girl standing in the sea just here, on Sandymount Strand, offering Stephen a poignant image of the reciprocal inspiration between himself and Ireland's imaginative consciousness. Worse, when yet another woman impinges upon his anxious doubts he reads her as a portentous emblem, only to misinterpret the import of his own reading.

Stephen's attention is drawn to a gypsy woman trudging down the beach, and he senses that if "Loose sand and shell-grit crusted her bare feet," too, nonetheless, she has "Tides, myriad-islanded, within her, blood not mine, *oinopa ponton,* a winedark sea. Behold the handmaid of the moon" (*U,* 48). This passing stranger incarnates the two halves of Stephen's impossible dichotomy: she struggles the straitened route of history with her path across the seawrack, but has the freedom of the sea within her. Like Eve, she is the source from which the tides originate, creatrix and servant alike of the forms of the past. Stephen's misconception is only in his retreat from this double existence under the stress of his alienation. Perhaps it is the fearsome female image that persuades him to miss his own cue about the interaction of past and present, micro- and macrocosmic seas, because in explicating *Hamlet* Stephen will incarnate the sea again in a direction much more in keeping with the aesthetic destiny of his D'Annunzian Icarus: "the sea's voice, a voice heard only in the heart of him who is the substance of his shadow, the son consubstantial with the father" (194).[63] In any case, what Stephen has missed, Bloom is now ready to discover as they, father and son, patriarch and student, move toward recognition.

Blood and heart as the voice of the sea bring us again to the "Sirens," an episode threaded with casual images drawn from the sea, as well as those more crucial ones we have noticed: the barmaids with "moist" hands, with "wet" and "coral" lips, Simon Dedalus singing "to a dusty seascape," the bar become a "reef," the "oceansong" Lydia hums. And the narrator binds the imminent action more decisively to Stephen's seaside meditations of the morning when Bloom not only catches up the association of numbers, cords, and communication, but does so in a context that echoes Eve and "Edenville." The refrain "all is lost now" runs through Simon's ballad, of course, and is echoed in the "All gone, All fallen" of "The Croppy Boy." A tailor is drawn in only that the narrator may tell us his shop is at "number five Eden quay" (*U*, 274).

And the symbol of Stephen's sense of the past as dead and deadly has been waiting as a mute but central prop from the opening pages of "Sirens": "Miss Douce halfstood to see her skin askance in the barmirror gildedlettered where hock and claret glasses shimmered and in their midst a shell" (*U*, 254).

The flirtation of a barmaid and a customer exposes Bloom to a banal scene that his psychic commentary will convert into the wisdom of *Ulysses* sifted from that of the kabbalah. The man has coyly been wooing the barmaid who, still quite full of a seaside vacation, brings her souvenir seashell into action: "She had a gorgeous, simply gorgeous, time. And look at the lovely shell she brought. To the end of the bar to him she bore lightly the spiked and winding seahorn that he, George Lidwell, solicitor, might hear.—Listen! she bade him" (*U*, 275). Holding it to his ear, Lidwell "heard," this last reminding us of the human vocal cords, "Wonderful, more than all the others" in song. The shell sings, counterpart to the voice, while Bloom hears its song in imagination as Lidwell and the barmaids literally listen alternately.

> Bloom through the bardoor saw a shell held at their ears. He heard, more faintly that that they heard, each for herself alone, then each for other, hearing the plash of waves, loudly, a silent roar. . . .
>
> The sea they think they hear. Singing. A roar. The blood is it. Souse in the ear sometimes. Well, it's a sea.
>
> Corpuscle islands.
>
> Wonderful really.
>
> (*U*, 276–77)

Bloom in "Lestrygonians" had given a shudder of unconscious agreement to the signatures of death which Stephen had read in the shells as seawrack on the strand. In serio-comic consonance with the micro-macrocosmic interdependencies of the novel's symbols and theme, Bloom projected his intestinal strains into the vast image of a dying universe: "Gasballs spinning about, crossing each other, passing. Same old dingdong always. Gas, then solid, then world, then cold, then dead shell drifting around" (*U,* 163). Here the shell is a universal history of dead forms. But in listening to the listeners at the Ormond Bar, Bloom is drawn through the conch shell to articulate a realization not shared by Stephen. Stephen seeks only to free himself from the cords to his past, with which timidity makes him feel strangled, while Bloom sees that the past is always being made alive through the third ear of the microcosm. The shell waits, holding its message from the past ("Akasic" memories: 141). The sea within vivifies the greater seas without, recapitulating its "singing." And when Stephen ultimately learns to view the relationship of micro- and macrocosm in this way, learns that the past is not a dead hand upon the present if the present breathes life into the past, he awakens from the nightmare view of history. It will be Bloom who will instruct him, and the instruction will come, inevitably, as Hebraic song.

After Bloom paternally determines to protect Stephen in the maternity hospital where the birth of Mrs. Purefoy's boy elicits an elaborate context of fertility rites and emblems and drunkenness, there is the confused aftermath in Bella Cohen's brothel, where Bloom assumes growing authority. Then, in the small hours of the night, the voyagers return to the kitchen on Eccles Street, spent with the fantasies of Nighttown, the British soldiers, the protean sailor, and the guardrail behind the house. On every hand history, the past, has risen in twisted specters: in the linguistic evolution of styles descriptive of Mina Purefoy's birth pangs, the ghoulish metamorphoses of the elder Dedaluses, of little Rudy, of Paddy Dignam and the grey rat, in the half-mythic figure of the probable (but only probable) Skin-the-Goat, getaway driver for the Invincibles, walking actor from a murder drama that had become ancient Dublin history.

But now all is calm, and there are numerous indications that we are to recognize the climax of a paternal search in this meeting where the pair become "Bloom Stoom" and "Stephen Blephen" (*U,* 666), "each contemplating the other in both mirrors of the reciprocal flesh of theirhisnothis fellowfaces" (687). The entire colloquy by catechism is permeated by water imagery, by talk of telegraphs and numbers—by the meaningful matrix shared separately by Stephen and Bloom in "Proteus" and "Sirens." Then comes that moment in which the ultimate mystery of paternity is revealed as patriarchal, generative in the sense that Bloom's name carries at the beginning of the *Zohar:* that of teacher. History teacher; teacher of history as idea and destiny, the reality of experience as the conscience of a race. Setting out as Dedalian artist, the young Stephen had glimpsed the need for idea, ideal being reencountered in the imagination for the millionth time that it might be recreated. But returned from that self-exile with which *A Portrait* closed, the Stephen who walks along the strand in "Proteus" has closed himself off from family, friends, and that Ireland the expression of which is his aesthetic destiny. During their nocturnal travels he has fended off Bloom's anxious range of advice, proposals, and schemes with a near silent withdrawal that recalls so many of his encounters with others, from his alter-image student, little Sargent, to Buck Mulligan. But as Bloom persists, Stephen finally offers some chanted fragments of that language he has spurned, the Gaelic of his race's past. Hearing Bloom's reciprocal performance, Stephen suddenly bursts through the self-imposed barriers to grasp Bloom's insight in that simplest and most significant dimension, what he has called experience. The dead past comes alive suddenly, proved upon his pulses. As Bloom chants a Hebraic anthem, "What was Stephen's auditory sensation? He heard in a profound ancient male unfamiliar melody the accumulation of the past" (673).

V

Let us now return to the kabbalistic tradition. "The world of action," explains Mathers, "[is] called also the world of shells . . . *Alahim Ha-Qliphoth,* which is the world of matter. . . . In it is also the abode of the evil spirits which are called 'the shells' by the Qabalah."[64] The conception of shells as receptacles at once containing and distorting the higher *sephiroth* Mathers once put succinctly into an explanatory note: "the 'shells' . . . are the demons in whom again is a form of the Sephiroth, distorted and averse."[65] It is Waite, though, who shows us how this symbol is related explicitly to the marital and generative failure of the Blooms which originated in Molly's vision of the copulating dogs:

> . . . descent into manifestation . . . is the path of Shekinah, and when it is testified that she was destined from the beginning to suffer with Israel this means that the nuptial intercourse which was infinite and holy in the world above, which was pure, spiritual and holy for a period . . . in the world below, descended through what is termed the Fall of man into the region of the shells, or the order of animal things.[66]

But this is also Stephen Dedalus' world of the shore (on which "lies poor dogsbody's body" [*U,* 47]) and the past: "An old pilgrim's hoard, dead treasure, hollow shells" (30). Further, we find the other half of Joyce's symbolic antinomy almost inevitably in the world of the *Zohar,* where, as a modern scholar says, "The process of life in God can be construed as the unfolding of the elements of speech,"[67] or, as Waite put it, one accepts the "Mystery of Union between the Voice and the Word."[68] This other half is Bloom's psychic and symbolic metamorphosis of the dead conch-shell into aural life, a metamorphosis that bridges the distinction between micro- and macrocosmic reality. "From this ear [of Microprosopus, the created man] depend the highest Arcana," translates Mathers, "which go not forth without, and therefore is (*this* ear) curved in the interior parts, and the Arcana are concealed therein."[69]

To understand the importance of the aural in *Ulysses* we have turned to that moment in the night at which Stephen's "auditive sensation" was that "He heard in a profound ancient male unfamiliar melody the accumulation of the past." To understand its importance in the *Zohar* we must turn to the treatment of *Binah,* the third *sephira,* since she draws into conjunction another of the principal symbols of both the kabbalistic literature and *Ulysses:* the sea. Here in the kabbalah is the prototype for Bloom's revivifying union of past and present, shell and sea through the modality of the ear, and for Stephen's initial mistake about history, personal and public, being a nightmare, a mistake that Bloom's aural lesson corrects.

From the unity of the first *sephira, Kether* (the undifferentiated, ancient One) there issues as an initial duplication the masculine potency 'wisdom [Chokmah].' Next there issues the third *sephira,* which Mathers describes as "*Binah,* the Understanding, who is co-equal with *Chokmah.* . . . She is the supernal Mother . . . also sometimes called the great sea."[70] Mulligan alludes in admiration to "our great sweet mother" (*U,* 7) as he looks off the Martello tower, but this opening scene also sets up an ambivalence toward the mother sea when Stephen reacts by recalling his mother's death and coalesces the two in "a bowl of bitter waters" (11), the bile and tears of her wracked body and psyche.[71]

The sea, though, is also life as it is identified with Molly, to whose womb Bloom returns symbolically to rest, and who has been literal mother to Milly and Rudy. It is doubtless a commonplace of exegesis to observe that as her grand affirmations of sex are made beside the ocean at Gibraltar and upon the hill of Howth, so at the moment of the novel's action her menstrual flow is "pouring out of me like the sea anyhow" (*U,* 754), "that awful deepdown torrent and the sea the sea crimson sometimes like fire" (768). Again, the micro- and macrocosmic seas are united, but now in the aura of that great mother who shares Molly's birthday and name, permitting Joyce to build into the Christian pun upon Mary-*mare* aspects of *Ulysses.* Mathers had interpolated that equation into the *Zohar:* "The forms of Chokmah and Binah . . . are summed up in Aima the great Mother . . . identical with the Catholic custom of invoking the intercession of the Virgin with her Son; for Mary=Mare=Sea; and the Great Sea is Binah."[72] And as the "Greater Holy Assembly" explains, that part of the beard of Macroprosopus[73] which arises from the heart "hath dominion over and descendeth and ascendeth in sixty-nine thousand authors of grief. . . . And by that conformation all those are subjected, and mitigated in the bitterness of tears, which become sweet in the great sea" (as Mathers adds, "By the great sea Binah, the third Sephira, is probably meant".)[74] This pattern is echoed in the created world inasmuch as in the eyes of Microprosopus "abide two tears, and when He . . . desireth to have mercy . . . then He sendeth down those two tears so that they may grow sweet in the (waters of the) great sea . . . which is that of excellent wisdom."[75] And, like Joyce, Mathers, remembering the syncretic tendency of the Christian kabbalists in the Renaissance, suggests that the supernal mother's "exaltation into Binah is found in the Christian assumption of the virgin."[76]

Mathers's translation of the kabbalistic literature and Waite's commentary upon it, then, anticipated Joyce in a symbolic superstructure that is at first thought entirely obvious. The sea as life-giving and the shell as historical aftermath are naturalistic and therefore nearly universal symbols. But their double existence in an epistemological act in which sea, shell, ear, and knowing are drawn together as instruments for the individual's reconciliation with the macrocosm is Joyce's particular debt to and edification of reading in now-strange texts.

As George Lidwell holds the conch-shell to his ear in the Ormond Bar with the aid of the willing siren Lydia Douce, Bloom, we recall, comments to himself: "The sea they think they hear. Singing. A roar. The blood is it. Souse in the ear sometimes. Well, it's a sea. Corpuscle islands" (*U,* 277). Receiving knowledge and receiving the historical flow of life within oneself by ear are the same: that is the lesson Stephen is schooled in by his Jewish teacher Bloom (Hugh Kenner found Dublin, above all, a verbal city, and Molly Bloom is a singer). But Bloom perhaps learned it from the earlier patriarch of the *Zohar* who concluded, "Therefore concerning the ear it is called hearing; but in this hearing, Binah, the Understanding . . . is comprehended; for, also, to hear, is the same as to understand."[77] But to hear and understand is to hear the word incarnate in the voice.

In the course of his difficult day Stephen passes from the rejection of history as a pedagogical burden in the classroom overshadowed by that anti-Semite Deasy to the epiphany of the past stimulated by Leopold Bloom's Hebraic chant, that Leopold Bloom who earlier realizes the power of "The human voice, two tiny silky cords. Wonderful. more than all the others. . . . It's in the silence you feel you hear. Vibrations" (*U,* 272). Again the kabbalistic literature can not only explain that the world of *beth* alone is our world and history our destiny and Stephen's, but also put that lesson into metaphors that help illuminate the cause for the communication between Bloom and Stephen occurring under a canopy of interstellar spaces which has so often been read with chilling pessimism. The kabbalists suggest quite the reverse: "From Negative to Positive . . . eternally vibrates the Divine Absolute of the Hidden Unity of processional form. . . . To the uttermost bounds of space rushes the Voice of Ages . . . and eternally that Voice formulates a Word which is glyphed in the vast ocean of limitless life."[78]

If one may read between the texts, between the lines of action and interpretation within the text of *Ulysses,* the voice is Bloom's, the word is *bereshith bara,* in the beginning—the word of *beth* and Adam, not of *aleph* and *Adam Kadmon.* And the gloss of Bloom's Torah has been sympathy and communion as it is possible among men: "Between the waters and the waters. (Since there are the superior) perfect waters, and (those which are in Microprosopus) imperfect waters (or those mingled with severities; because in another manner it is said) perfect compassion, imperfect compassion," is Mathers's way of putting it;[79] "meeting of the waters" (*U,* 160), said Joyce.[80]

VI

A kabbalistic coursing of the symbolic tradition structuring the narrative of *Ulysses* has resulted in a hopeful and humane sense of the future and its possibilities, a sense that reinforces the life-bringing difference when Elijah, incarnate as Bloom, is translated from the waste land of *Dubliners* into the Dublin of *Ulysses.* But some wariness is in order before we too flatly accept the optimistic assurance of the kabbalists that the divine voice glyphs the word in the image of Bloom. We know how much the confessional elements of Joyce's work owe to Augustine, and it is Augustine who, at the very midpoint of *The City of God,* seems to be rebutting both the *Zohar* and Bloom in a passage with echoes in both: "God speaks with a man not by means of some audible creature dinning in his ears, so that atmospheric vibrations connect Him that makes with him that hears the sound."[81] This warning comes as Augustine passes from his castigation of Rome and of the pagan gods to his distinction between that particularly successful commercial city[82] and the heavenly city of love. As such, his corresponds to that transition in which Malachi's warning closes the Old Testament and promises the New with the richly figural Elijah as bridge. And when Augustine comes to read this transitional passage itself, he recalls our awareness not only to Joyce's persistence in treating the city as spiritual metaphor, but to the double nature of metaphoric narrative (as Waite said of the kabbalah, "it is only as if casually that the word interpretation can be held to apply . . . the Secret Doctrine is rather the sense below the sense . . . as if one story were written on the obverse side of the parchment and another on the reverse side"). For instance: literal voice. Joyce seems to mock his own carefully constructed movement toward Stephen's sense of history heard in Bloom's Hebrew, seems to justify Augustine's warning about Truth not dinning in the ears by way of atmospheric vibrations, when Stephen immediately disrupts their communion by chanting to Bloom the old anti-Semitic ballad of the Jew's murderous daughter. It is ethnic and therefore all too literal, like the mythology of the murderous hangman in "Cyclops" which activates Bloom's Jewish claim upon Christ and humanity as "Love . . . the opposite of hatred" (*U,* 327).

So in one story Stephen wanders away toward a vague destiny, a sojourner in the city of carnal and commercial man who has rejected Simon Dedalus's, Buck Mulligan's, and Leopold Bloom's homes as mere momentary hospices. And Bloom sleeps with Molly perhaps to have eggs and sex in bed and another son ab ovo.

In his illuminating study Alexander Welsh says, "The good in Dickens are sojourners . . . in the literal sense of St. Augustine and St. Paul. They are travelling beyond the earthly city, beyond death."[83] This is both true and not true of the young artist and Mosaic traveling salesman of *Ulysses,* a doubleness paradoxical in distinguishing Joyce's modernism from his Victorian legators by way of his adaptation of an older hermeneutic. In *Dubliners* the Dantesque allusions and structures had trapped the citizens in an infernal city. In *A Portrait* the escape was putative, based in the transcendent flight promised in old mythologies revived. In *Ulysses* both stories are told at once. Bloom and Stephen walk the earthly city represented by Dublin with their respective dreams of the East ironically acknowledged as failure (Paris: "seabedabbled, fallen . . . Lapwing") or fantasy ("Agendath Netaim"). But they exist elsewhere, too. As we have begun to understand in great detail, the protagonists of *Ulysses* contribute to the voice and vision of the narrators without fully sharing them. Indeed, Bloom at the end is less aware of his complicated relation to Moses or any patriarch than Stephen had been of his problematic relation to his namesake, "the fabulous artificer," in *A Portrait.* The most knowledgeable bibliographer of the book concludes that "Joyce wanted *Ulysses* to be a record of all the stages he passed through. . . . The processes seem to me to support readings of *Ulysses* that emphasize its ambiguity, which in this case seems best defined as a desire to hold opposing meanings or values in permanent suspension. . . . This progression meant a shift from a verisimilitude to symbolism and from the characters to the schema. But Joyce retained his entire range of concerns in the final version."[84]

This conclusion supports our confidence in reading another story written on the "reverse side" of the Dublin day with the symbolic code of the kabbalistic texts so profoundly influential upon Joyce and Yeats. And if one allows this same sensibility to two simultaneous texts to draw him back to that other metaphoric interpreter of the city, St Augustine, he reconciles himself hermeneutically with the Jewish kabbalists, using (ben Bloom) Elijah as vehicle:

> For not without reason do we hope that before the coming of our Judge and Saviour Elias shall come, because we have good reason to believe that he is now alive; for, as Scripture most distinctly informs us, he was taken up from this life in a chariot of fire. When . . . he is come, he

> shall give a spiritual explanation of the law which the Jews at present understand carnally, and shall thus "turn the heart of the father to the son." . . . And the meaning is, that the sons, that is, the Jews, shall understand the law as the fathers, that is, the prophets, and among them Moses himself, understood it.
>
> (XX,xxix)

It was the *Zohar* that offered Joyce "Bloom" as the name for the patriarchal teacher of that Irish son who had once petitioned "Old father, old artificer, stand me now and ever in good stead." It was the Hebrew prophet Malachi who would identify him not as Dedalus but as that other fiery charioteer of the sun, Elijah. It was the false prophet Malachi Mulligan who would tempt Joyce's artist-avatar Stephen to delimit his book as mere mythic rather than mystic fiction: "Hellenise it" (*U,* 9).

V

HELIOPOLIS

I. *Futurism*

Scarcely had Joyce mastered the historico-mythic persona and form sired upon Sir Arthur Evans's Cretan discoveries by D'Annunzio when D'Annunzio exiled himself to France and was immediately challenged by his rebellious Italian emulator, Filippo Tommaso Marinetti. Early in 1909 *Le Figaro* published Marinetti's *Manifesto of Futurism,* which is set within an all-night symposium of young poet-artists and which reads like nothing so much as a page from some fevered diary of a D'Annunzian protagonist such as Stelio Effrena. "Mythology and the Mystic Ideal are defeated at last." "We stand on the last promontory of the centuries. . . . we will destroy the museums, libraries, academies of every kind." In their place, the futurist will celebrate "multicolored, polyphonic tides of revolution in the modern capitals," will celebrate the airplane, the racing car. "Museums: cemeteries! . . . Identical, surely, in the sinister promiscuity of so many bodies unknown to one another."[1]

Two years later Marinetti attacked D'Annunzio directly for having distilled from his talent the poisons that futurists must eliminate: "Obsession with lust and its eternal triangle of adultery seasoned with the pepper of incest and the stimulating spice of Christian sin," along with "the profound passion for the past." Three decades later, just such a charge might be laid against

Finnegans Wake, that history which opens upon the museyroom as necropolis. Yet styles complicate; aesthetic rejections and developments interlace confusingly in these years. For *Finnegans Wake* might equally stand as the triumphant epitome of what Futurism offered to replace D'Annunzio's model:

> the Futurist poets sought to convey the "simultaneity" of impressions which characterized modern life. The stylistic devices by which they sought to achieve this aim were the abolition of traditional syntax, metre and punctuation and the introduction of mathematical and musical symbols, onomatopoeia and "free expressive orthography . . . freely deforming, remodelling the words by cutting or lengthening them . . . enlarging or diminishing the number of vowels and consonants."[2]

Coincidence is not usually quite that, of course. If *Finnegans Wake* could by hindsight seem to reflect these aspects of futurist poetics, historical perspective also sees that, for all of Marinetti's violent epistles to the English and for all of Wyndham Lewis's disclaimers, Vorticism and Futurism seemed to the objective eye twin energies sired upon the thrust of novel perception offered by Cubism.

The immensity and ephemerality of the occasion have forever swallowed what it meant to the imagination of individual men to pass over on that one Parisian night into a new millenium, the twentieth century. But it is clear that in the first years following that moment when these young Italians forged the "manifesto," the collective imagination of Europe was in the process of adapting to every variety of ahistorical "futurism," to a new grasp of continuities reduced to myths of new beginnings rather than of origins.

Bellamy's *2000 A.D.* gave way to Wells's *War of the Worlds;* Captain Nemo was triumphing over New Jerusalem mythologies that had dominated futuristic literature from Virgil onwards; Wagner was giving way (Marinetti's 1914 "Down with the Tango and Parsifal") to Luigi Russolo's complex sound machine for producing *Intonarumori;* radio and the movies were establishing a beachhead against the book only to find experimental television appearing on the horizon. A potential new stage for dismissing old stages of civilization. "Systematically prostitute all of classic art on the stage," Marinetti advised, "performing for example all the Greek, French, and Italian tragedies, condensed and comically mixed up, in a single evening." This would be the aim of the new drama of sequins and klieg lights: "The Variety Theater, born as we are from electricity, is lucky in having no tradition, no masters, no dogma."[3]

Finnegans Wake would include the variety theater as a principal stage, as it would include Joyce's homage to all of this post-historical world of a generalized "futurism" in its incorporation of radios, races, and gunboats, in the large celebration of that newest experimental eye upon instant history, television.

But too, given James Joyce as its author, *Finnegans Wake* is a Victorian book in that its society is familial (incestuous, as Marinetti feared), its locus the city. And, as always, the city was Dublin. And, as always, Dublin only as a center upon which was laminated the idea of the city as symbol of history. And, if Irish history, then ancient history; the exact new dimension in which the old Joycean equation would this time be explored was suggested long before he dreamed of this last manifestation. As a desperate effort at self-support, Joyce had lectured to an Italian adult education group in Trieste in 1907 on "Ireland, Island of Saints and Sages." An obvious and provincial subject, he briefly managed to broaden it in a way that would be prophetic of his final universal mythology: "The religion and civilization of this ancient people, later known by the name of Druidism, were Egyptian."[4]

II. *Coincidences*

The letters of those months following the publication of *Ulysses* are painful in every sense, revealing James Joyce at his worst. Nora left for Ireland, a separation veiled as a visit. Stanislaus also attempted a break, finally articulating his sense of James's ingratitude. Sylvia Beach and Joyce began their split over the issue of editions of *Ulysses;* Joyce temporarily alienated

Budgen on much lesser grounds. His eyes were (also temporarily) deteriorating, and operations loomed beyond the painful application of leeches. But the deepest source of distress (or was it a quintessential reflection?) can be seen in the creation of the "Scribbledehobble" notebook, a vague, almost superstitious recapitulation of triumphs past, as each early work, each chapter title for *Ulysses,* headed up pages that Joyce obviously hoped would form themselves into a new rhetorical structure on the analogy of Aristotelian commonplaces.

A first coincidence at this time might have shaken Joyce the mystic, had either he or its author-subject been aware of it.[5] Marinetti was born and raised in Egypt. In 1922, apparently oblivious of *Ulysses,* he published *The Untamables,* an allegorical novella about the desert, about African soldiers, Platonic prisoners of the sands, about the paper people who wore books for caps, words for gowns. It is a strange manifesto from the oasis overwrought in the way of that D'Annunzio whom Marinetti exorcises in a preface written to oppose a view of traditionalism which unwittingly evokes and embraces *Ulysses:* "Before us, men had always sung as Homer did, with narrative sequence and a logical catalogue of events, images, and ideas. There is no substantial difference between Homer's poetry and Gabriele D'Annunzio's. Our free-word tableaux, on the other hand, finally distinguish us from Homer since they no longer contain narrative sequence, but rather the simultaneous polyexpression of the world."[6]

Egypt had been no secret, of course. Stephen in *A Portrait* had experienced fear and pride as a putative avatar of "Thoth, the god of writers, writing with a reed upon a tablet and bearing on his narrow ibis head the cusped moon" (493). And Stephen had visualized Moses gathered to Pharoah's daughter even before the oratory in "Aeolus." From Blavatsky to Mead and Waite the spiritualists and scholars of the Hermeticism that impinged upon the edges of Kabbalah had probed the mysteries behind the pyramids.

And Joyce's psyche belonged to an age in which a tangible past impinged upon the imagination more strongly than any abstract forecast of the future. That much had been proven by

Schliemann's effect upon D'Annunzio, by the impact of Evans's Cretan excavations upon Joyce. Now, as the frustrated author of *Ulysses* thrashed about for a new project, it was thrust upon him from that ancient land which had been birthplace to the father of futurism, Marinetti. The news came forth first in the year that had given birth both to Marinetti's Egyptian novella and Joyce's Graeco-Hebraic-Irish masterpiece. On December 9, 1922, the *Illustrated London News* announced, "Last week, Lord Carnarvon and Mr. Howard Carter revealed what has been described as promising 'the most sensational Egyptological discovery of the century'—the finding of the complete funeral paraphernalia of King Tutankhamen . . . [who] reverted to the ancient cult of Amen Ra."[7]

Another waste land had given up its secrets so vividly that the past could once again be seen and felt as a presence, as before at Troy and Mycenae. But the coincidences did not end in this lucky imaginative chance. The Egyptian tomb was a mere way-station, a posthouse on the way back that led from the necropolis to the metropolis. And the metropolis of the Gods, of Amen-Ra, was, like Dublin's Phoenix Park, Heliopolis. When he read about it, one wonders whether Joyce remembered Bloom's journey through Glasnevin hades and "back to the world again. . . . They are not going to get me this innings. Warm beds: warm fullblooded life" (*U,* 113). Certainly he must have smiled at coincidence to recall how Bloom, contemplating the passing of cities "worn away age after age," had recalled Herodotus' account of the "Pyramids in sand. Built on bread and onions" (162).

The stimulation to the author in search of a structure was immediate: "Joyce seemed very interested in the religious aspects of Tutankhamen's tomb, which we discussed shortly after its discovery on 26 November 1922," according to Arthur Power, the young Irishman in Paris whom Joyce had made into something of a recalcitrant companion-protégé in the months girdling the publication of *Ulysses.* Power's explanation for this interest offers a glimpse into how Joyce saw his latest projected version of the *felix culpa* as a return to *A Portrait* in the sense that this work would constitute the new *Metamorphoses* on a larger scale than either Joyce or D'Annunzio had earlier dreamed of inventing. It was to be a history of the world as nature's continuum: its protagonists a hill, a river, an ant, a grasshopper, a donkey, a hen. He reportedly told Power:

> Whenever I walked through the British Museum . . . I was always impressed by the . . . Egyptian monuments . . . those Egyptian figures of birds and cats. It always occurred to me that both the Assyrians and the Egyptians understood better than we do the mystery of animal life, a mystery which Christianity has almost ignored, preoccupied as it is with man. . . . I cannot remember at the moment a sympathetic mention of a dog or a cat in the New Testament. . . . It is true that the parable of the lillies of the field touches on a deeper note, but one wonders why that parable was not taken further, and why the great subconscious life of Nature was ignored.[8]

Throughout the following months and years the archaeological news continued to come in. Photos and color reproductions of the chests, the chariots, the mummy masks, abounded; imaginative drawings flooded the popular journals for a decade, as had the Minoan materials a quarter-century earlier. As with D'Annunzio's projection of Schliemann's emotions into *La città morta,* as with the cultivated union with ancient mysticisms which formed the context for turn-of-the-century kabbalism, the immensity of impact that the Egyptian recoveries had upon Joyce and his coevals was that of an unmediated engagement that went far beyond mythologies in laminating present and past in a single presence. I cite somewhat at length Howard Carter's account of first looking into the tomb of Tutankhamen for its poignant sense of that copresence which seems a peculiarly anguishing need for so many acute imaginations of Joyce's generation:

> At first I could see nothing, the hot air escaping from the chamber causing the candle flame to flicker, but . . . as my eyes grew accustomed to the light, details of the room within emerged slowly from the mist, strange animals, statues, and gold. . . . For the moment—an eternity it must have seemed to the others standing by—I was struck dumb with amazement, and when Lord Carnarvon, unable to stand the suspense any longer, inquired anxiously, "Can you see anything?" it was all I could do to get out the words, "Yes, wonderful things." . . .

> For the moment, time as a factor in human life has lost its meaning. Three thousand, four thousand years maybe, have passed and gone since human feet last trod the floor on which you stand, and yet, as you note the signs of recent life around you—the half-filled bowl of mortar for the door, the blackened lamp, the finger-mark upon the freshly painted surface, the farewell garland dropped upon the threshold—you feel it might have been but yesterday. The very air you breathe, unchanged throughout the centuries, you share with those who laid the mummy to its rest. Time is annihilated by little intimate details such as these.[9]

Again, as in D'Annunzio's earlier play about the excavation of the dead city which incorporated it as a part of, a party to, psychic events in the present, we hear, and Joyce heard more poignantly, the romanticism of archaeology. And if it had earlier been a science that had offered mythic materials for *A Portrait,* it was to become (it seems justifiable to extrapolate from the *Ulysses* schema, given the evidence of "Scribbledehobble") the "art" of *Finnegans Wake,* that book excavated from, made over in the metaphor of, that archaeological mound, the mud heap. But if the archaeologists had followed the mappings of previous digs ultimately to Tutankhamen's tomb in the Valley of Kings, it *was* a tomb, not, as at Troy or Mycenae, a dead city. The city was elsewhere, the city of Heliopolis. But it was in the tomb that one found the ancient Baedeker by which Joyce could resurrect Dublin in the image of its ancient counterpart. Coincidences. That Phoenix Park should have its nominal mythic origin in the sunbird of the Egyptian city of recovered souls was one more. It was the one that Joyce needed to realize that an old fascination connected early with the kabbalah and late (coincidence again) with a big book inherited by a friend in Paris offered the form for a new history of the world. It is as though the Egyptian excavations triggered all that had been forming in Joyce's imagination as mystic truth over the entire course of years that had given him *A Portrait* and *Ulysses.* Archaeology was to be the art; Phoenix Park was to be the old/new origin and end; the resurrection myth would recur under the "technic" of "drama." The protagonist would be not only the artist, but his creation, the book and its characters. The Egyptian spirits were, of course, supplied with their own guide book through the underworld of the tombs to Heliopolis. Its myriad forms were a subject of scholarly and mystic study that seemed almost as fascinating as the kabbalah for Joyce's earlier contemporaries around the turn of the century. Joyce's own early readings in it had been prophetic of the dramatic structures in *Finnegans Wake*. In 1912 in Trieste he had kept a notebook for lecturing in Italian on the history of English drama. Most of his notes were from the contemporary authorities A. W. Ward and E. K. Chambers. But a jotting on the drama's "religious origins" departs from these sources to incorporate Joyce's interpretation of what he had read in E. A. Wallis Budge's translations: "Egypt—Book of the Dead (persons: the Dead & the Gods)."[10]

III. *Book of the Dead*

"We left the flat together and walked over the bridge to the left bank. Joyce tapped the pavement repeatedly with his new snakewood stick. . . . He suggested that I should write an article on *Finnegans Wake* and entitle it James Joyce's *Book of the Dead.* We dawdled cityward."[11] Written just after Joyce's death, this is Frank Budgen's account of Joyce's insistence upon the importance of the Egyptian tomb guide that would lead Joseph Campbell the mythologist to suggest that it was laid under tribute in *Finnegans Wake,* [12] would lead to Atherton's quarrying of allusions in his study of structural books contributive to Joyce's conceptions,[13] and finally to a full monograph on the cycle of Osiris in the *Wake.*[14]

If Joyce did suggest an Egyptian essay to Budgen, it was probably owing not only to Budgen's *transition* essay on Norse elements in 1928,[15] but also to Joyce's frustrated hope of Harry Crosby doing part of a successor volume to *Our Exagmination* (into which the Norse essay had been incorporated). Joyce wrote to Harriet Weaver early in 1929: "I am planning . . . a book of only 4 long essays by 4 contributors (as yet I have found only one—Crosby—who has a huge illustrated edition of the *Book of the Dead,* bequeathed to him by his uncle)" (*L,* I, 281). Six months later Crosby committed suicide. The "huge illustrated edition" was probably E. A. Wallis Budge's "facsimile," with translation of the Papyrus of Ani, issued by the British Museum in 1895. Late in his life Budgen reported to Atherton that he had seen Joyce studying the popular three-volume edition of the *Book of the Dead* into which Budge had incorporated other recensions as well as this centrally significant version.[16]

The excitement about Tut's tomb undoubtedly reinforced, if it did not revive, Joyce's earlier interest in Egyptology. It was an interest that sealed the mythico-historical reality of a cultural palimpsest. A. E. Waite would acknowledge the palimpsest casually in the final words of a preface with which he introduced his redaction of the two earlier books on the kabbalah in 1929, as Joyce was laying groundwork for Crosby's advertising the Egyptian element in the *Wake* and Crosby was instead preparing for suicide. Waite wrote:

> If SEPHER HA ZOHAR is not of time immemorial but belongs to the 13th century, which almost certainly it does not in the root-matter, my investigation is not stultified. There remains the question of values, the question of life and essence. . . . if the strange tale of a Garden, with which Genesis opens, holds something within it which belongs to the spiritual deep, . . . it signifies little enough if the figurative myth concerning the Fall of Man is a century or an age later than the BOOK OF THE DEAD.[17]

It was an old configuration, no doubt restimulated in the aging scholar-mystic as it had been in Joyce by the spectacular archaeological discoveries. A small fragment of pseudo-history appears in a footnote to Mathers's *Kabbalah Unveiled:* "Apart from the sacred ideas we attach to Amen, it is well to know that the ancient Egyptians called their greatest Deity *Amen,* AMN, Amen-Ra, and Ra=Light, AVR in Hebrew; Amen our Light, the light of the two countenances."[18]

This little note of philological legerdemain reflects a continuing excitement among the members of the Golden Dawn about the syncretism of Eastern religions. No sooner had the

Mathers gone into Parisian retreat than Yeats found himself being reluctantly pushed out of sympathy by Moina Mathers's dashed off notes about being "plunged in 'Egypt.'" In the winter months of 1900 and 1901 he had to deal with Florence Farr Emery's invitation into her incipient rebel group of any member of the Order feeling sympathetic interest in "the study of the Egyptian Book of the Dead." Small indicators are, as so often, the best keys to a psychological milieu. A significant part of the *Book of the Dead,* of course, is given over to the naming formulae at each pillar and postern in the mastabah tomb through which the soul must pass on its way to the resurrection into the day at Heliopolis. The Temple vault in the London quarters of the Golden Dawn was a gaudy emblematic mixture more reminiscent of Blavatsky's *Isis Unveiled* than of Budge's *Osiris,* but it was not meant to reflect the Egyptianism of the Mathers. So it was that during the crisis of revolt within the Order at the turn of the century, Marcus Worsley Blackden failed the advanced adept examination because he had been preoccupied with translating from the "Book of the Dead for the Lecture on the Pillars."[19] If Egypt never triumphed in the terminology of London, we should remember that the Edinburgh Temple of Amen-Ra initiated nearly fifty members into the Golden Dawn in half a dozen years of the late nineties.[20] And Amen (Atem)-Ra was to become, along with Shem the Penman, protagonist of *Finnegans Wake.*

IV. *Atem, Shem, and the Rubbish-Heap*

There is no need to recount or expand upon the catalogues of entries made into *Finnegans Wake* by the kings and gods of Egyptian mythology or their impingement upon the Continental European imagination through Bruno in the Renaissance and Vico in the eighteenth century, two authors whose systems have doubtless not been exaggerated as structural influences upon the *Wake.*

Let us in these closing pages rather focus upon the mysteries and mythologies of the artist and his art in the figures of father and son. It is where Joyce began as the boy looked up at the old priest's window in "The Sisters," it is the paradox at the root of Daedalus/Icarus, of Bloom/Stephen. It is the interaction that closes Joyce's mythologies with Atem and Shem in alliterative pairing.

Shin (שׁ) plus Mem (מ) equals Shem (שׁם). The name of Noah's son, but primarily a sign, a token, a mark; hence, a name. The internal essence outwardly revealed; hence, all names of Jehovah. Thus, for instance, it is understood from Fuerst's *Hebrew and Chaldee Lexicon of the Old Testament.*[21] The spirit made letter, then. A buried missive come to light as the creator reveals himself metaphorically.

In the internal structure of *Finnegans Wake* the singularity and universality of Shem as letter and name are reconciled in his writing the letter that is the book from and upon himself. It is Joyce's final reprocessing of self from death to life (a recycling begun with Icarus' double sense of destiny) through art's forging the consciousness of a race. His Shem, after all, is an Irish forger of the *Book of Kells,* the Gospels spun out as Irish art, as the new scripture.

But we recognize that the historical dump in which the enigmatic letter of *Finnegans Wake* is found always reappears on the landscape in the company of allusions to the ritual formulae of the tomb papyri as well as to Atem-Ra's peculiar creative activities at the site of Heliopolis. This leaves a nagging and key question of imaginative transfer and cohesiveness: if the womb-tomb of civilization derives in significant part from Joyce's reading about Egyptian primeval myths of the mudhill and the elaborately constructed burial vaults, what leap induced him to transform it into the "old dumplan" of "festering rubbages" picked over by Kate and the hen? The answer is implicit in a little book that floated into the currents of popular culture in 1916 and was soon forgotten in itself, but that was so pertinently pilfered, parodied, and cross-grafted by Joyce that we may justifiably assume it is the "structural book," to employ Atherton's useful distinction, for that crucial recurrent center of *Finnegans Wake,* the "fatal midden or chip factory . . . (dump for short)" (110).

There is irony and a parable of humility for scholars in the circumstances of the author's dubious immortalization in *Finnegans Wake,* since he, James Hope Moulton, was an eminent and versatile classical scholar, professor of New Testament Greek at Manchester University as well as governor of the John Rylands Library.[22] But he was also a Wesleyan clergyman with a strong interest in evangelical and missionary work, and the book Joyce saw was the product of this side of Moulton's activities, of the breezy evangelical popularizing that had been the target of Joyce's satiric barbs from the first in the not-very-fictitious Father Purdon or Alexander J. Dowie.

Like the letter of *Finnegans Wake,* Moulton's message came from Massachusetts, originating happily in lectures to a Christian missionaries' commemorative meeting in Northfield, the home and burial place of Dwight Lyman Moody, the American evangelist who appears in *Finnegans Wake* coupling irreverently with his colleague Ira David Sanky as "Sankya Moondy" and "Missioner Ida Wombwell" (60: see also 533: "First Murkiss, or so they sankeyed"). But this Joyce would not have learned until he opened to the preface, and certainly the title alone was sufficient to function as both challenge and catalyst to his genius for metamorphosing the absurd into art. For with the smug cleverness of a Christian salesman making religion come alive for plain folk (the book was, Peake observed, "full of interesting facts, brightly presented"), Moulton, quondam meticulous author of a *Prolegomena to a Grammar of New Testament Greek,* titled his little book *From Egyptian Rubbish-heaps.*[23] Joyce quite possibly never read beyond the first lecture, since nothing from the others peeps through in the text of the *Wake,* although some of the names and anecdotal trappings offered tempting opportunities he would have been unlikely to pass up altogether. Yet that first lecture on "Egyptian Rubbish-heaps and the Study of the New Testament" was rich enough to offer a valuable new perspective on the Egyptian materials Joyce had quarried from the *Book of the Dead.*

The argument of Moulton's lecture was rooted in his lifelong scholarly effort to demonstrate that the vocabulary and style of the New Testament were not unique, but were based in the nonliterary vernacular Greek of the first century, that it "is the only book written in the language of daily life, in the very language in which the people talked at home."[24] And to explain how his thesis was verifiable, Moulton enlightened his audience on the manner in which archaeology had collected the unself-conscious ephemeral documents of New Testament times.

"What is the nature of them and where do they come from?" Moulton asks, a question that sets the pattern for I, v, of *Finnegans Wake,* even as its answer anticipates that of Joyce's exegete: "Well, to begin with, they come from rubbish-heaps. It seems to have been the custom in Egypt in the olden days not to burn waste paper, but to dump it outside of the town, and then let the sand of the desert sweep over it. Egypt, you remember, is the country where it hardly ever rains. It is out of this sand that we get these documents, perfectly fresh after thousands of years."[25] Moulton goes on to conjure up a layered stockpile of casual history even more casually accreted:

> Now this paper when it was done with was, as I have said, simply thrown away. The sand came up and covered it. Another layer of paper accumulated, and the sand covered that also. . . .
>
> In these rubbish-heaps you will find all the kinds of writing you would expect to find in sacks of waste paper collected down street nowadays. In one house there is a lawyer's office; lower down there is a shop; next door a private house. Farther on we pass a school, a church, a court-house, the government offices, and so on. Suppose waste paper collected from all these, you can picture the very large variety of documents included, and will see how many characteristics of our modern life they would illustrate, especially if among them there are many private letters, from people of all ages and degrees of culture. Now that is exactly what we have got in these Egyptian rubbish-heaps.[26]

But then, Moulton explains, the Egyptians' ways were not our ways, and much of the surviving documentation is in unexpected form, just as the letter of *Finnegans Wake* is characterized surprisingly as "a genuine relique of ancient Irish pleasant pottery" (111):[27]

> There is one other kind of writing material which you would not think of. The ancient pottery was generally not glazed, and it took

> writing very well. . . . Suppose a piece of it dropped and smashed into a dozen fragments. These fragments were saved, and when the mistress of the house wanted to send a note to a friend, or when the master wanted to send a receipt, or a bill, or a cheque, a fragment of broken pottery was used for the writing: and we have today multitudes of these *ostraca.*[28]

Here is the germ of thc "gnarlybird agathering" the fragments of quotidian history on the dump when the letter motif is first introduced into *Finnegans Wake:* "all spoiled goods go into her nabsack: curtrages and rattlin buttins, nappy spatees and flasks of all nations, clavicures and scampulars," items through which she steals "our historic presents from the past post-prophetical" (*FW,* 11). And at the next return of the motif, Kate Strong, having nosed "old dumplan" and found it full of "rotten witchawubbles, festering rubbages and beggars' bullets, if not worse" (79), "left down, as scavengers, who will be scavengers must, her filthdump near the Serpentine in Phornix Park" (80).[29] When the letter finally is unearthed, it is by the rootings of the "cold fowl" scratching upon "that fatal midden . . . (dump for short)" (110).

There remains the fact that the rubbish-heap of *Finnegans Wake* is also the "Mastabatoom" into which that fragmented protagonist HCE has been laid, or rather, has created of himself with the shells of his own fall, gathering the ubiquitous Humpty-Dumpty ("if Humpty shell fall frumpty times" [*FW,* 12]) into the mythologies of old Egypt. The first mastabah tomb allusion sets the Egyptian tone for each recurrence. When Kate Strong is gathering, we hear of "those pagan ironed times . . . when a frond was a friend inneed to carry, as earwigs do their dead, their soil to the earthball" (79), a reminder that HCE's "crested head is in the tropic of Copricapron" (26), the scarabaeus who wraps his world-egg in dung. It is, of course, this rubbish-heap of HCE's making from which the hen finally scratches up the letter from Boston (Mass.) (anagrammatic echo of the tomb), which is also the *Book of Kells* and, hence, their prototype and culminating version, *Finnegans Wake* (which explains why the author of the exegetical description of the manuscript identifies himself as "a tombstone maker" [113]). Moulton provided, as I have suggested, the unexpected but critical connection between rubbish-heap and tomb:

> But I must tell you that these documents come from other places as well, and particularly from tombs. The tombs of ancient Egypt are the places from which in all ages men have been recovering relics of antiquity. The ancient Egyptians . . . had a very strong belief . . . that when the man was put in the grave it was necessary for him to be provided for in every way. Especially it seems to have been thought necessary that he should have his favorite reading; so they buried with him copies of the books he loved to read. I am afraid we have very unkindly taken away large numbers of these books, which repose in our libraries today.[30]

And although we know how almost literally Joyce parodied in paraphrase long passages of Sir Edward Sullivan's account of the *Book of Kells* manuscript in the exegete's meticulously scientific description of the letter's physical state,[31] some of the parodic elements are at least equally aimed at Moulton's irrelevant and heavy playfulness as a scholar slumming in the purlieus of the eager uninformed. When the exegete carefully catalogues the "original sand, pounce powder, drunkard paper or soft rag used" (*FW,* 114) in the rubbish-heap letter of *Finnegans Wake,* his maker seems to be remembering Moulton's explanation that "these documents are written upon the paper of antiquity. Our word *paper* is, as you know, taken from the word *papyrus* . . . I might tell you the way in which this writing material was made. They used a papyrus plant," and so onward *ad absurdum* through the processes of stripping, rolling, and drying the matter buried in the sands of time.[32]

Finally, if the "paper wounds" described by the letter's analyst reflect Sullivan's explanation of ancient Irish punctuation, they bring the examination of the document to a close in a context that again is Egyptian through the allusion to Moses in the bulrushes: "on holding the verso gainst a lit rush this new book of Morses responded most remarkably to the silent query of our world's oldest light and its recto let out the piquant fact that it was but pierced but not punctured (in the university sense of the term) by numerous stabs and foliated gashes" (*FW,* 123–24).

Joyce's suggestion that the light of Egypt reveals the mutilation of the Irish manuscript echoes the Irish simile in Moulton's gay account of the tattered papyri of Egypt: "Papyrus is very brittle, and a great many of these documents are remarkably like the Irishman's coat, of which it was said that it mostly consisted of fresh air. When you have documents consisting mainly of holes—when you have a few holes and then a few words and then more holes, it takes a great deal of skill to be able to read them; but it is perfectly marvelous how highly trained observers can read things not there."[33] This is in the spirit of Shem's serious shamming. And it matters because, while extending the fusion of high and low styles which reconstitutes the notion of rhetorical decorum in *Finnegans Wake,* the allusion subordinates the *Book of Kells* to passing parity with an Egyptian "scripture" consonant with the creation myth dominating the recurrent contexts of the letter that is also avatar of "James Joyce's Book of the Dead," as he had alluded to it in the conversation with Budgen.

But by way of this buried and lacerated letter from the dead, let us return to the origin of the necropolis that is also the resurrection city of the sun, Annu, Heliopolis, where "wee dead walkner" (*FW,* 170). To do so is to return to the epigraph from Lewis Mumford's work with which this book's first chapter was introduced. It was cited in conjunction with Bloom's meditations in a mood of defeat which encompassed memories of Herodotus' observations on the magnificent futility of the pyramids. But Bloom knew better in other moods. He had passed from beneath the little cloud that made Agendath Netaim seem a colony of the Dead Sea across the street and into the morning sun (his first going forth by day out of the tomb). More symbolically, if no less literally, he left the cemetery to reclaim that sun and his own life after his morbid imaginings at Paddy Dignam's burial (accompanied by all those meditations upon burying utensils Egyptian-style, gramophones and telephones by means of which we might communicate with the quasi-quondam dead).

Joyce begins his career with *Dubliners* depicting a Dantesque dead city and concludes with Dublin as the burial ground of HCE. It is, of course, another version of renewal, the palimpsest of fallen cultures rising anew, which echoes the smaller metamorphoses of classical and kabbalistic origin shaped into the myths of *A Portrait* and *Ulysses.* But now renewal is cyclic, universal, beginning in the natural symbiosis of hill and river, "swerve of shore to bend of bay," a universal naturalism that Joyce had noticed as an aspect of the Egyptian sense of continuities between man and animal and land when he commented to Power upon the Eastern garnerings in the British Museum. This, too, lies at the heart of the city, not only as Joyce mythologizes the Liffey and Phoenix Park and the Howth Hill in *Finnegans Wake,* but as the modern city reveals its origins in ancient outlines that emerge in the Egyptian and Jewish cultures that offered shape to his Irish *commedia.* Mumford speculated that "Mid the uneasy wanderings of paleolithic man, the dead were the first to have a permanent dwelling; a cavern, a mound marked by a cairn, a collective barrow." This ancient mound introduces us to the rubbish-heap as man's evolving museum at the beginning of *Finnegans Wake* through the proto-conversation of those prehistoric versions of man, Mutt and Jute. Bloom, of course, always looked east toward the Holy Land, the morning of his Gibraltar bride, of his race.

> Long ago the Jews claimed as their patrimony the land where the graves of their forefathers were situated; and that . . . claim seems a primordial one. The city of the dead antedates the city of the living. In one sense, indeed, the city of the dead is the forerunner, almost the core of every living city. . . . The first germ of the city, then, is the ceremonial meeting place that serves as . . . a site to which family or clan groups are drawn back, at seasonable intervals.[34]

But nowhere, of course, had the necropolis taken on such magnificent form as among the cemeteries of the Pharoahs which sprang upon the twentieth century's need for touch with the dead past as living fact, as evidence that history could prove one long and vibrant lamination of man's cultures upon his natural origins.

> The success of the first dynasties in evolving a religious form of government, centering in a king who was a living god, changed the problem of city building . . . it created a unique type of city, fully developed only in Egypt: the city of the dead. Around the central pyramids of

> Gizeh we find a veritable urban settlement of corpses with the tombs placed in orderly rows . . . the mastabas of nobles even have the appearance of houses.[35]

These historical observations draw us to Joyce's final myth of the creator as the Egyptian sun-god Atem-Ra in *Finnegans Wake,* and, by way of the mastabah tombs, to Leopold Bloom's masturbation.

In *A Portrait of the Artist as a Young Man* the image of a supererogatory artist-god was that of a supercilious dandy who, withdrawn from the world he had made, pared his nails. At the acme of supercilious and frightened pride with which he appears in the early pages of *Ulysses,* Stephen leaves excrement as his sign: "the dry snot picked from his nostril. . . . For the rest look who will" (*U,* 51). At his most creative moment, Mr. Casey, defender of the fallen Parnell, spit in the "drunken old harridan's" eye ("*O Jesus, Mary and Joseph!* says she. *I'm blinded! I'm blinded and drownded!*" [*PA,* 279]). Bloom shits in the morning, masturbates in the evening. Shem ("with his penname SHUT sepiascraped on the doorplate"), "exceeding in violent abuse of self," "made synthetic ink and sensitive paper for his own end out of his wit's waste" (made "any quantity of obscene matter . . . through the bowels of his misery" [*FW,* 183–84]). He is writing the letter buried in the dungheap, "over every square inch of the only foolscap available, his own body, till by its corrosive sublimation one continuous present tense integument slowly unfolded all . . . cyclewheeling history (thereby, he said, reflecting from his own individual person . . . a dividual chaos, perilous, potent, common to allflesh, human only, mortal)" (185–86).

The stuff is always sterile in appearance, excrement. Perilous, common, but the primordial matter before one psychoanalooses oneself, before mythologies begin to individuate into story. Dead and fertile like the scarab dungbeetle of the Egyptians who rolled the world into being; excremental and vivifying. Like a book based upon sound puns from more than a dozen languages yet based too in the literal scratchings we call, Joyce called in *Finnegens Wake,* the "letter." In his literary or literal phase, the traveler toward Heliopolis in the *Book of the Dead* proclaims: "I have brought the inkpot and the palette as being the objects which are in the hands of Thoth; hidden is that which is in them. Behold me in the character of a scribe! I have brought the offal of Osiris, and I have written thereon."[36]

In the economy of the *Book of the Dead* everyman becomes Osiris; Osiris is resurrected in every man. But Osiris is an avatar of Shem, of Icarus, of the son. As such, he is also avatar of the artist, spouse of Isis, poet of the vilanelle. He inhabits the created world of *Beth,* and so is not the creator whose act begins all mythologies of origin: Alpha, Aleph, Atem. One critic has reduced Stephen Dedalus' metaphysic to a formula that can help us survey the dilemma of the corpus: "to copulate is human, to masturbate divine."[37]

Viewed from such a perspective, Bloom's onanism is only surface vehicle for Stephen's antisocial fear. It is, from a different perspective, a costly prelude, as Moses' disbarment from promise in the kabbalistic complex behind *Ulysses* suggests, as Bloom's long exile from Molly's loins proves. But much more costly has been Stephen's self-absorption, and it is this isolation from which the Egyptian mythology offers a spectacular vehicle of escape. Or rather inversion. But it is, of course, only a vehicle, and, if a principal one, only one among many that form the sense of life in *Finnegans Wake.* Yet perhaps it is more instructive than the others in that it resonates with all the mythologies and Victorian visions that went before.

Let us recollect it in its simplest outlines. They are divinely excremental:

> The ancient Egyptian texts contain many allusions to spitting. . . . Under certain circumstances it was considered to be a creative act. Thus when, according to a legend which is as old at least as the Pyramids, the god Tem had had union with himself he spat, and his spittle was the gods Shu and Tefnut.[38]

> The god Temu once in Heliopolis took the form of a man who masturbated. He thrust his phallus into his hand and worked it about in it, and two children, a brother and a sister, were produced, Shu and Tefnut.[39]

Finnegans Wake is a literal cube of sight and sound so that the spitting could be incorporated into more forms than ptah and ptuh (411, 413, 590), although these are important manifestations of deity, as Henri Frankfort reminds us: "even Atum, generally worshipped as the creator of gods and cosmos, is but an emanation of Ptah."[40] Yet from beginning to end it is masturbation upon which *Finnegans Wake* centers language and plot, not least owing to its coincidental echo of mastabah tomb. It begins with Finnegan's "stuttering hand," variates into jokes that incorporate the creative excrement of the scarab dungbeetle[41] ("in fancymud murumd. . . . He stottered from the latter. . . . Mastabatoom, mastabadtomm, when a mon merries his lute is all long" [6]), and constitutes a thread throughout the book which always draws one back to the rubbish-heap with its "onanymous letters."[42]

Shot semen, spit, shit. They have all become creative excrement like the letter itself. In *Ulysses* Joyce had focused his mythology largely on the prophets insofar as it constituted a creative gospel, as in *A Portrait* he had delimited it to an inventor and his son. With the universal embrace built into the form of *Finnegans Wake* he could replace the artist with the gods as earlier he had tried to replace the gods with versions of the age-old mythology of the artist as creator. Now it was more natural, a relaxation from myth into a way of being back home in two senses. The first sense was what Joyce had felt a long time before when he realized that "the Egyptians understood better than we do the mystery of animal life." The dogs of *Ulysses* were Hebraic symbols, images of evil; the cat was a reflection of Molly's selfishness reflected in the mind's eye of Bloom as much as it was a reflection of Bloom's generosity in our own. But *Finnegans Wake* turns brothers into ant and grasshopper, man and wife into hill and river, the latter running incestuously back into the father-husband ocean. It is this last act of metamorphosis which returns *Finnegans Wake* and Joyce's long enterprise to its familial beginnings, turns the most modern text back to its Victorian genesis. For finally here—not by way of the titular drunken hod-carrier's fall, nor Man's in the edenic paradise lost in Phoenix Park, nor in the broken images gathered from classical culture—here Joyce found the hymn that would reconcile those wary prototypes of father and son he had imaged in "The Sisters" and whose desperate metamorphoses he had traced through the dead cities of other mythologies. Perhaps it was right, just right, in the end, that this strangest and final one should incorporate a sterile onanistic gesture and the necropolis into origins of the family. If he implied its inevitability in "The Sisters," Joyce voiced the cyclical longing in Bloom's musings upon Paddy Dignam's funeral and what death means to women in the human family: "Extraordinary the interest they take in a corpse. Glad to see us go we give them so much trouble coming" (*U,* 86).

Joyce was an old-fashioned man and writer of many languages and mythologies, always sensing how he had wanted to be back there where he had begun. And only able finally to still the jokes that contribute even to the close of *Finnegans Wake* in the adaptations of Egyptian images and a woman's voice. It was a last acknowledgment that the mythic syncretism, the reassembling into renewed order of the dismembered parts of man's history, was really a symbol for man's paradoxical and persistent renewal under the rubrics of both nature and art.

Osiris, accused, dismembered, floats upon the waters that carry him away then return him to Isis. But he, like HCE, was once judged in the Great Hall of Heliopolis. He, too, was accused and calumniated by Set "until at length Thoth silenced him and made clear the innocence of Osiris."[43] Stephen Dedalus had been moved by a "sense of fear of symbols and portents . . . of Thoth, the god of writers, writing with a reed upon a tablet and bearing on his narrow ibis head the cusped moon" (*PA,* 225). He need not, as the author of *Finnegans Wake* knew. In the later trials of all men and women, all incarnations of Osiris, Thoth's son Anubis had been more severe than his father: "the care which he displayed in scrutinizing the . . . Balance, and his obvious anxiety lest the heart should gain any advantage to which it was not legally entitled, make it quite clear that the deceased could expect no favour." But the father had not forgotten us: "Close by the Balance . . . stood the ibis-headed god Thoth, holding his reed and palette, and he watched the weighing of the heart of the servant of Osiris as carefully as he watched the trial of Osiris himself."[44]

Anna Livia grown old and renewed sums up less her own diminishing life than Joyce's knowledge that these are the terms common to us all, antique or not: from Heliopolis to necropolis and back again by way of a long voyage. "It's Phoenix, dear" (*FW*, 621) is a conclusion more mystic and yet more realized than all its longer mythic metamorphoses as Joyce struggled to sense and say how old he and the enterprise of making it all new were. How amorphous, androgynous, endlessly repetitive: "How you said how you'd give me the keys of me heart. . . . But you're changing, acoolsha, you're changing from me, I can feel. Or is it me is? . . . First we feel. Then we fall. . . . old it's sad and weary I go back to you . . . my cold mad feary father . . . and I rush, my only, into your arms. I see them rising. . . . Carry me along, taddy, like you done through the toy fair" (627–28).

It is a passage in which the changes upon life and death, childhood and age return vividly to the language and structure of *A Portrait*, which begins in the innocent embraces recounted in babytalk and courses through the weary sophistication of Stephen's experience into his final embrace of a fortunate fall in acceptance of a father who is perhaps less Dedalus than Thoth the scribe. And it returns us also to *Ulysses*, that other account of the encounter of father and son in which Stephen and Bloom both deepen their personal and our mythic understanding that "the accumulation of the past" is an ocean in which we need not fear drowning if we accept its "washup" as baptism into the continuing stream of life.

Introductory to Anna Livia's last rush back into the arms of the sea, the washerwomen of *Finnegans Wake* sum up Joyce's spiritual journey in familiar terms which he might have accepted as epigraph for any sympathetic encounter with his mind experienced through his written corpus:

> "the book of the Depth is. Closed. Come! Step out of your shell!" (*FW*, 621)

NOTES

Chapter 1

1. Alexander Welsh, *The City of Dickens* (Oxford: 1971), brilliantly develops the Victorian emergence of the family/city relationship:

> The problem was in many ways unanswerable: the future of individual life, as of the city, was obscure. Confronted with this problem, however, the nineteenth century developed a homely remedy of its own—so snug, so cherished, so endlessly invoked, that we are apt to discount its importance. . . . No writer was fonder of exploiting this contrast than Dickens; if the problem that besets him can be called the city, his answer can be named the hearth. . . . What the hearth signifies for Dickens is primarily the family. . . . Relations with family and friends are the only relations in the city that are not commercial.
>
> (pp. 142, 144)

Tony Tanner, *City of Words: American Fiction, 1950–1970* (New York, 1971), pp. 116–40, 202 ff., isolates the structural use of the city by Burroughs and Hawkes.

2. *L,* I, 55. Joseph K. Davis, "The City as Radical Order: James Joyce's *Dubliners,*" *Studies in the Literary Imagination,* 3, no. 2 (1970), 79–96, summarizes and supplements earlier critical remarks on Joyce's sense of the city.

3. Arthur Hugh Clough, "Review of Some Poems by Alexander Smith and Matthew Arnold," in *Prose Remains,* ed. by his wife (London, 1888), p. 359 (first published in *North American Review* in 1853).

4. George Gissing, *The Nether World,* cited in J.A.V. Chapple, *Documentary and Imaginary Literature, 1880–1920* (New York, 1970), p. 96.

5. Virginia Woolf, "The String Quartet" (originally published in *Monday or Tuesday* [1921]), in *Haunted House* (London, 1944), pp. 22–27.

6. In Chapple, *Documentary and Imaginary Literature,* p. 96.

7. See Hugh Kenner's interesting statistics on the growing popularity of the "Temple" Dante between 1899 and 1906: *The Pound Era* (Berkeley, 1972), pp. 76–77.

8. Compare Angelina Da Piana, *Dante's American Pilgrimage* (New Haven, 1948), pp. 133–39, and Harry W. Rudman, *Italian Nationalism and English Letters* (London, 1940).

9. "The Voyage," sec. I in *Poems and Some Letters of James Thomson,* ed. Anne Ridler (Carbondale, Ill., 1963). All quotations from Thomson are drawn from this edition.

10. William D. Schaefer, "The Two Cities of Dreadful Night," *PMLA*, 77 (1962), points out that in all three extant manuscripts this Dantesque epigraph is present, while the reinforcing epigraph from Leopardi is not (p. 612).

11. Ibid., pp. 609–15.

12. Florence L. Walzl, "Gabriel and Michael: The Conclusion of 'The Dead'," *JJQ*, 4 (1966), 17–31, persuasively argues that both readings are correct; that Joyce built into the ending an ambiguity reflecting a gradual shift in his attitudes. Here I will argue for a definitive choice only within the context of *Dubliners.*

13. Richard Ellmann, *James Joyce* (New York, 1959), p. 226.

14. Howard Helsinger, "Joyce and Dante," *ELH,* 35 (1968), 591–92.

15. Wyndham Lewis, *Blasting and Bombardiering* (1937; 2d rev. ed., Berkeley, 1967), p. 235.

16. Stanislaus Joyce, *My Brother's Keeper* (New York, 1957), p. 228.

17. "The order of the stories is as follows. *The Sisters, An Encounter* and another story which are stories of my childhood: *The Boarding-House, After the Race,* and *Eveline,* which are stories of adolescence: *The Clay, Counterparts,* and *A Painful Case* which are stories of mature life: *Ivy Day in the Committee Room, A Mother* and the last story of the book which are stories of public life in Dublin" (*L,* II, 111).

18. For the fragment of a manuscript for *A Portrait* and Joyce's allusion to it in the Pola Notebook (1904), see Robert Scholes and Richard M. Kain, eds., *The Workshop of Daedalus* (Evanston, 1965), pp. 85, 107–8.

19. A pioneering debt is owed to Brewster Ghiselin ("The Unity of Joyce's *Dubliners,*" *Accent,* 16 [1956], 75–88, 196–213) who, while forcing patterns erratically, genuinely established the "unity" that Levin and Shattuck ironically brought into question in their early botched attempt (Richard Levin and Charles Shattuck, "First Flight to Ithaca: A New Reading of Joyce's *Dubliners,*" *Accent,* 4 [1944], 75–99).

20. See also the comments on the bazaar as a Dantesque Hell in Ben L. Collins, "Joyce's 'Araby' and 'Extended Simile,'" *JJQ*, 4 (1967), 88–90.

21. The clearly structural nature of these "winter" allusions is emphasized by external evidence. The "Araby in Dublin" charity bazaar for the Jervis Street Hospital was held during the spring (May 14–19, 1894). This

season would be more appropriate for a story of early pubescent love, of course, were the story intended to stand alone, a point unlikely to be overlooked by Joyce whether he was remembering a childhood disappointment or working from the flier distributed for the affair (see Ellmann, *James Joyce,* p. 40, and the advertisement reproduced opposite p. 80).

22. With the exception of "A Mother," which has no indication of season.

23. The relevant passage in "The Sisters" was added to the story for the collection, not appearing in either the *Homestead* or surviving (intermediate?) manuscript version: "In the dark of my room I imagined that I saw again the heavy grey face of the paralytic. I drew the blankets over my head and tried to think of Christmas. But the grey face still followed me" (11).

24. One recalls "the bottle-green eyes" of the pervert of "An Encounter" (27).

25. The candle-lighting passage was the major addition to the *Irish Homestead* version of the story: see Robert Scholes and A. Walton Litz, eds., *"Dubliners": Text, Criticism and Notes* (New York, 1969), p. 242.

26. Nor does this Dantesque pattern, of primary significance to the function of the story within the structure of *Dubliners,* exhaust Joyce's maneuvering. A convincing argument has been made for a detailed Homeric parody by Nathan Halper, "The Boarding House," in *James Joyce's "Dubliners": Critical Essays,* ed. Clive Hart (New York, 1969), pp. 72–83.

27. For the *Irish Homestead* text see Marvin Magalaner, *Time of Apprenticeship: The Fiction of Young James Joyce* (New York, 1959), pp. 174–80, and for the surviving manuscript, James Joyce, *Dubliners,* ed. Scholes and Litz, pp. 243–52. For a different set of ironic developments of Christian allusion in the revisions see Peter Spielberg, "'The Sisters': No Christ at Bethany," *JJQ,* 3 (1966).

28. Magalaner, *Time of Apprenticeship,* pp. 80–81.

29. For the relevant correspondence see *L,* II, 142–85 passim, and Robert Scholes, "Grant Richards to James Joyce," *Studies in Bibliography* (Charlottesville, 1963), 16:139–60.

30. *Last* in this phrase means last completed, not final position: on March 13, 1906, Joyce indicated that the new story "is to be inserted between *The Boarding House* and *Counterparts*" (*L,* II, 131). See also Florence L. Walzl on the revision: "Joyce's 'The Sisters': A Development," *JJQ,* 10 (1973), 375–421.

31. On Little Chandler as poet and Joyce's self-conscious projections in that role see James Ruoff, "'A Little Cloud': Joyce's Portrait of the Would-be Artist," in *Research Studies of the State College of Washington,* 25 (1957), 256–71.

32. Gallaher's coalescence of sexual and religious secrets in strange lands is owing to such scriptural accounts as this: "Then did Solomon build a high place for Chemosh, the abomination of Moab, . . . and for Molech, the

abomination of the children of Ammon. And likewise did he for all his strange wives, which burnt incense and sacrificed unto their gods" (I Kings 11:7–8).

33. It is in this role that he makes his one appearance among the pages of *The Golden Bough,* I, 258, and Frazer expatiated upon it in *Passages of the Bible Chosen for their Beauty and Interest* (London, 1909), pp. 476 ff.

34. The larger analysis of the complex relationships between *Ulysses* and *The Waste Land* has been variously developed without reference to the particular Elijah context from Giorgio Melchiori, *"The Waste Land" and "Ulysses," ES,* 35 (1954), 56–68, through Stanley Sultan, *"Ulysses," "The Waste Land" and Modernism* (Port Washington, 1977), pp. 14–28. Sultan summarizes as well as develops tracings of Eliot's debt. He also notes the use of Dantesque allusion in a "waste land" context shared by Joyce and Eliot (pp. 35–41).

35. T. S. Eliot, *The Complete Poems and Plays, 1909–1950* (New York, 1962), p. 50. All citations are from this edition.

36. *L,* I, 231 (August 15, 1925). For two somewhat erratic accounts of Eliot's largely "subconscious" or "unconscious" borrowings from *Ulysses* see Thomas M. Lorch, "*Ulysses* and *The Waste Land,*" *Texas Studies in Language and Literature,* 6 (1964), 123–33, and Robert Adams Day, "Joyce's Waste Land and Eliot's Unknown God," in *Literary Monographs: Volume 4,* ed. Eric Rothstein (Madison, Wisc., 1971), pp. 137–210, 218–26. On Joyce's sense that Eliot had cannibalized *Ulysses* see pp. 187–88 and 224 nn. 105 and 106.

37. B. L. Reid, *The Man from New York: John Quinn and His Friends* (New York, 1968), p. 405.

38. In the *Little Review* version of "Telemachus," Joyce had emphasized the bond between Stephen and Bloom at this early hour before their meetings with phrasing that was removed, doubtless because it was inappropriate to Stephen's pithier early style. "A clod [*sic*] began to cover the sun slowly, wholly, shadowing" in *LR* became "A cloud began to cover the sun slowly, shadowing." It has been convincingly argued that the promise of renewal is implicit for Stephen as for Bloom, by way of symbols from contemporary *Haggadah* accounts of Passover, an argument that dovetails into the Jewish emphasis of chapter 4 below (see Daniel Mark Fogel, "Symbol and Context in *Ulysses:* Joyce's 'Bowl of Bitter Waters' and Passover," *ELH,* 46 [1979], 710–21).

39. Lewis Mumford, *The City in History* (New York, 1961), p. 53.

40. The fishing up of Dodd's son from the Liffey owes nothing to Eliot or to Weston; the episode is in the *Little Review* version of "Hades" (September, 1918) as well, of course, as in the *Egoist* version (July, 1919).

41. History sometimes seems to have conspired to give Joyce his symbols ready-made. Ellmann (*James Joyce,* pp. 38–39) authenticates the

incident as one that happened in 1911 to Dodds, the senior Dodd having been a moneylender to whom John Joyce was heavily in debt.

Chapter 2

1. C. P. Curran, *James Joyce Remembered* (New York, 1968), pp. 105–15. Robert Scholes and Richard M. Kain have quoted translations from this novel and *Il fuoco* in *The Workshop of Daedalus,* pp. 269–79. These are among the more extravagantly dithyrambic D'Annunzian flights of egotistic exaltation of the artist, and they are more pertinent to the first prose-poem version of "Portrait" and the posings of obiter dicta of *Stephen Hero* than to *A Portrait.* A similar emphasis is developed more extensively by Robert M. Adams, "The Operatic Novel: Joyce and D'Annunzio," in *New Looks at Italian Opera,* ed. William W. Austin (Ithaca, 1968), pp. 260–81. It was quite other aspects of D'Annunzio's work which fed into the mature *A Portrait.*

2. Ellmann, *James Joyce,* p. 78.

3. Long in the possession of Curran. See *James Joyce Remembered,* p. 9.

4. Ellmann, *James Joyce,* p. 80.

5. Gabriele D'Annunzio, *Poesie, Teatro, Prose,* ed. Mario Praz and Ferdinando Gerra (Milano and Napoli, 1966), pp. 85, 469.

6. *L,* II, 76, 80. In light of the primarily dramatic interest Joyce exhibited in D'Annunzio as well as in Ibsen at this period, George Russell's statement that Joyce told him in 1903 that he was "writing a comedy which he expects will occupy him five years or thereabouts" becomes doubly tantalizing (Scholes and Kain, *Workshop of Daedalus,* p. 166).

7. Joyce, *My Brother's Keeper,* pp. 166–67, is amusing on Joyce's infatuation with the actress, to whom he sent some adulatory verses that were never acknowledged. Emilio Mariano, *Sentimento del vivere ovvero Gabriele D'Annunzio* (Verona, 1962), pp. 105–24, explores the complicated (and self-serving) maneuverings among Bernhardt, Duse, and D'Annunzio which led to *La città morta,* and lays to rest the myth of it being motivated by D'Annunzio's passion for la Duse.

8. Hugh Kenner has illuminated the imaginative impact of the Trojan excavations without reference to D'Annunzio in "Homer's Sticks and Stones," *JJQ,* 6 (1969), 285–98.

9. From the text in *Istituto nazionale per la edizione di tutte le opere di Gabriele D'Annunzio,* ed. Angelo Sodini (Verona, 1929), II, 48. All citations are from this text; translations are my own.

10. The ambivalent suggestions Anna makes concerning Bianca Maria's love for Alessandro (1:1; pp. 19–21) closely parallel the confrontation between Bertha and Beatrice in act three of *Exiles* (95–98).

11. As we will see, D'Annunzio later (in *Il fuoco*) interprets this as a cry of triumph over nemesis, a "grido della luce." But see Giovanni Getto, "La città morta," *Lettere Italiane,* 24 (1972), 45–96, especially 53.

12. "Ibsen's New Drama" (1900), in *The Critical Writings of James Joyce,* ed. Ellsworth Mason and Richard Ellmann (New York, 1959), pp. 47–67.

13. *E,* p. 112. See the argument for doubt as structure in John MacNicholas, "*Exiles:* The Argument for Doubt," *JJQ,* 11 (1974), 33–40. See also Getto's apt description of the world and mood of *La città morta:* "D'Annunzio gathers his sources into a new and organic unity, into a play of silences and shadows, into interrogations and trepidations, of absences and inexorability, from which rises a suspended and sorrowing music" ("La città morta," p. 58). In 1919 *Exiles* was placed on the schedule of the Stage Society along with *La città morta,* only to be removed under pressure from G. B. Shaw (Ellmann, *James Joyce,* p. 429).

14. Cited in Pietro Scotti, "I 'Giornali' della crociera Dannunziana in Grecia (1895)," in *L'Arte di Gabriele D'Annunzio: Atti del converno internazionale di studio,* 7–13 October 1963 (Verona, 1968), p. 650.

15. Ibid., p. 651. For Scotti's speculations upon the trip's provision of dubious detail in the play, see pp. 658–61.

16. *Taccuini,* ed. Enrica Bianchetti and Roberto Forcella (Verona, 1965), pp. 61–72.

17. Guy Tosi, *D'Annunzio en Grece: "Laus Vitae" et la croisiere de 1895 d'apres des documents inedits* (Paris, 1947).

18. Getto, "La città morta," p. 90, details D'Annunzio's search for the French translation of Schliemann's book by way of his friend Georges Herelle in Paris.

19. Henry Schliemann, *Mycenae: A Narrative of Researches and Discoveries at Mycenae and Tiryns* (1880; reprint ed., New York, 1967), p. 147. In light of the earlier discussion of Bloom/Elijah as rain-maker in "Hades" and this role's fulfillment in "Oxen of the Sun," it is interesting to reinforce Joyce's participation in a Victorian psychological set toward mythic neosyncretism by quoting Schliemann's further remarks upon the chapel: "And it appears likely that the very site of the present open shrine of the prophet Elias was in ancient times occupied by a sanctuary of the sun-god, who had celebrated a cultus there, and who has given way to the prophet Elias, with hardly any change in the orthography or pronunciation Eelios. This is a wonderful coincidence" (p. 147).

20. The fountain was actually seen by D'Annunzio and his fellow travelers, but its name was probably borrowed from Schliemann (*Mycenae,* pp. 59–60): see also Scotti, "I 'Giornali' della crociera Dannunziana," p. 657.

21. Mason and Ellmann, *Critical Writings,* p. 71.

Chapter 3

1. See Homer Obed Brown, *James Joyce's Early Fiction* (Cleveland, 1972), pp. 107–31, on the remaking of both projects at this juncture.

2. Ellmann, *James Joyce,* p. 274.

3. Ibid., p. 275. Joyce refers to "The Day of the Rabblement."

4. Stanislaus Joyce, *My Brother's Keeper,* pp. 166–67. Curran, *James Joyce Remembered,* pp. 106–13, elaborates this observation by Joyce's brother mistakenly, I think, by tracing it in the character of Stephen Dedalus in *A Portrait.* Curran's 1962 essay in *Studies* was not acknowledged in its adaptation by Scholes and Kain, *Workshop of Daedalus,* pp. 242, 269–79.

5. All page references to *The Maidens of the Rocks,* trans. Annetta-Halliday-Antona and Giuseppe Antona (Boston, 1902).

6. Scholes and Kain, *Workshop of Daedalus,* p. 242.

7. *Stephen Hero,* p. 99. The American editions all have *expending,* corrected to *expanding* in the Jonathan Cape edition, p. 104.

8. A summary of popular views is offered in Lanfranco Orsini, "D'Annunzio e Wagner: per un riesame del cosidetto dilettantismo Dannunziano," in *L'Arte di Gabriele D'Annunzio,* ed. Emilio Mariano (Verona, 1968), pp. 133–38.

9. In reality, when he wrote the novel and parted from Duse, D'Annunzio was thirty-five, she was forty. The novel suggests a woman of forty, but a man much younger—it is a mythic portrait of the artist as a young man passing just across the barrier into aesthetic maturity.

10. The labryinth that so stirred Stelio Effrena's mythic imagination and that plays so large a structural role in *A Portrait* was a persistent symbol for D'Annunzio: see E. Giachery, *Verga e D'Annunzio* (Milano, 1968), pp. 193–310.

11. A thorough survey of the wide publicity and public appeal of the Cretan discoveries, as well as a detailed version of their relevance to *A Portrait,* is available in Diane Fortuna, "The Labyrinth as Controlling Image in Joyce's *A Portrait of the Artist as a Young Man,*" *Bulletin of the New York Public Library,* 76 (1972), 120–80.

12. July 26, 1902, cited from Fortuna, "Labyrinth as Controlling Image," p. 125.

13. Gabriele D'Annunzio, *Il fuoco* (Milano, 1909); see also "Giorgione rappresenta nel' arte l'Epifania del Fuoco" (p. 97).

14. Harrison, p. 515, cited from Fortuna, "Labyrinth as Controlling Image," p. 129.

15. Gabriele D'Annunzio, *Le faville del Maglio* (Milano, 1928), II, 171–72.

16. All citations of *Alcyone* are from *Poesie, Teatro, Prose,* ed. Praz and Gerra. Translations are my own. The lyrics cited are on pp. 322–23; *Ditirambo IV* is cited by line number.

17. *Poesie, Teatro, Prose,* pp. 85, 137. Mary T. Reynolds, "Joyce and Dante" (manuscript), comments upon Joyce's deepened sense of Dante through the mediation of D'Annunzio from 1904 through 1907 (pp. 27–33).

18. Ibid., p. 158.

19. Julian B. Kaye, "Simony, the Three Simons, and Joycean Myth," in *James Joyce Miscellany, First Series,* ed. Marvin Magalaner (New York, 1957), pp. 20–36. It seems no accident in the context of father-son inversions of myth and role which Joyce shares with D'Annunzio that he should have chosen as the father figure Simon Magus, whose exposure came, like that of Ovid's early Icarus, through a fatal plunge from on high.

20. Fortuna, "Labyrinth as Controlling Image," pp. 175–76.

Chapter 4

1. Ellmann, *James Joyce,* p. 662.

2. Peter Demetz in his introduction to Walter Benjamin's *Reflections* (New York, 1978), p. xxii.

3. "The Author as Producer" (1934) in Benjamin, *Reflections,* p. 234.

4. Ellmann, *James Joyce,* p. 10.

5. Stuart Gilbert, *James Joyce's "Ulysses,"* (1930, New York, 1955), pp. 65–76.

6. The most detail is in Robert Tracy, "Leopold Bloom Fourfold: A Hungarian-Hebraic-Hellenic-Hibernian Hero," *Massachusetts Review,* 6 (1965), 523–38.

7. Ellmann, *James Joyce,* p. 562.

8. Ibid., p. 539.

9. Ibid., p. 562.

10. The nucleus of forgery and fraud passages are gathered in William York Tindall, *A Reader's Guide to "Finnegans Wake"* (New York, 1969), p. 138.

11. *Zohar,* I, 2b, trans. Harry Sperling and Maurice Simon (New York, 1928). Translations, unless otherwise noted, are from this edition compared with Jean de Pauly's French translation, which was available to Joyce at the turn of the century: *Sepher Ha-Zohar* (*Le livre de la Splendeur*) (Paris, 1906–1911).

12. Ellmann, *James Joyce,* p. 562.

13. *L,* III, 330–32; Ellmann's translation.

14. *Zohar,* I, 1b. See also de Pauley, *Le Livre de la Splendeur,* I, 5. Arthur Edward Waite, *Secret Doctrine in Israel* (London, 1913), translates "the flowers appear on the earth" (pp. 156–57). Knorr von Rosenroth's text (*Kabbala denudatae tomus secundus: id est Liber Sohar restitutus* [Frankfort, 1684], II, 154–55) reads as follows:

Isti sunt Patriarchae, qui ingressi sunt in cogitationem & ingressi sunt in mundum venturum, & occultati sunt in illo; & inde sunt in occultatione, & abscondit sunt in prophetis veritatis . . . . Et quis sustentat mundum, & causa est ut patres manifertentur? Vox puerorum, qui student in Lege, & propter illos justos mundi, mundus eripitur; id est, quod scribitur: *Ordines aureas faciamus tibi.* Cant. I,ii. Isti sunt pueri, adolescentuli mundi; sciut scriptum est: Et facies duos Cherubim (q.d. . . . juvenes, adolescentulos) aureos.

15. *The Holy Kabbalah* (London, 1929), p. 6. Joyce never relieves his symbolism from the corrective pressures of ironic perspective. Stephen and Bloom are characters primarily upon a narrative surface, and their relative callowness and superficiality are reflected explicitly in Bloom's lame command of his racial language and implicitly in the fact that the "ancient" melody is modern, being the opening lines of the (appropriately) Austrian-Hebrew poet Naphtali Herz Imber's *Ha Tikvah,* written in the nineties.

16. Samuel Schoenbaum, *Shakespeare's Lives* (Oxford, 1970), pp. 193–233.

17. Ibid., p. 360; see also pp. 332–61.

18. Richard Ellmann, *The Consciousness of Joyce* (Oxford, 1977), p. 122.

19. *Selected Poetry and Prose of William Blake,* ed. Northrop Frye (New York, 1953), p. 456. Marginalia to Wordsworth's poems.

20. Cited from John J. Dunn, ed., *Fragments of Ancient Poetry* (1760, Los Angeles: Augustan Reprint Society, Publication 122, 1966), p. v.

21. Alfred Nutt, *Ossian and the Ossianic Literature* (1899; 2d ed., London, 1910), pp. 89–90.

22. David Masson, *Chatterton: A Biography* (New York, 1899), pp. 303–4.

23. Adolf Rieth, *Archaelogical Fakes,* trans. Diana Imber (1967; reprint ed., New York, 1970), pp. 117–27.

24. See Ellic Howe, *Magicians of the Golden Dawn: A Documentary History of a Magical Order, 1887–1923* (London, 1972), pp. 233–72, and George Harper, *Yeats's Golden Dawn,* pp. 46–126.

25. William Butler Yeats, *A Vision* (rev. ed., 1956; reprint ed., New York, 1961), p. 12; see also p. 37.

26. Ibid., pp. 54–55.

27. William Butler Yeats, *Mythologies* (New York, 1959), p. 55 n.

28. The pamphlet "Is the Order . . . to remain a Magical Order?" is printed as appendix *k* in Harper, *Yeats's Golden Dawn,* pp. 259–68. Perhaps the essence of the difference in the two orders of "magic" represented by Mathers and Yeats is most succinctly apparent in a passage on their respective counterparts in one of the manuscripts of Yeats's "autobiographical" novel: "The difference of opinion about proper kind of symbolism . . . must be accentuated. Maclagan had better be quite definitely a disciple of the Rosy

Cross as that is embodied in the *Fama.* Michael should as definitely insist on the introduction of such a symbolism as will continue and make more precise the implicit symbolism in modern art and poetry. The antagonism must be made the antagonism between the poet and the magician" (William Butler Yeats, *The Speckled Bird,* ed. William H. O'Donnell, Yeats Studies Series [Canada, McClelland and Stewart, 1976], p. 226).

29. Harper, *Yeats's Golden Dawn* p. 100.

30. "Dead noise, Akasic records. All that ever anywhere was" (*U,* 142). See Gilbert, *James Joyce's "Ulysses,"* pp. 188–89, citing Sinnett's *The Growth of the Soul* on "the all but infinite memory of Nature, which is preserved with imperishable perfection in the all-embracing medium known to occult science as the *Akasa.*" Joyce directed Gilbert to the work of Sinnett, one of Madame Blavatsky's biographers and more sophisticated victims (Gilbert, *James Joyce's "Ulysses,"* pp. vii–viii). On Yeats's strong interest in Sinnett see Ernest Boyd, *Ireland's Literary Renaissance* (1916; rev. ed., New York, 1922), pp. 213 ff. Ellmann and other Yeatsian biographers have detailed Sinnett's Buddhistic influence upon the London Theosophical Society in the years before establishment of the Golden Dawn: see, for instance, Harper, *Yeats's Golden Dawn,* pp. 3, 5–6, and passim. It was here that Mathers lectured on the kabbalah as early as 1884.

31. William Butler Yeats, "Magic," in *Ideas of Good and Evil* (London, 1914), p. 46.

32. Leslie Fiedler, "Images of Walt Whitman," in *An End to Innocence: Essays on Culture and Politics* (Boston, 1955), p. 153.

33. Howe, *Magicians,* pp. 225–26.

34. Arthur Edward Waite, *The Brotherhood of the Rosy Cross* (London, 1924), pp. 568–84; see also Howe, *Magicians,* passim.

35. See Arthur Edward Waite, *The Doctrine and Literature of the Kabalah* (London, 1902), pp. 12–13, 307, and passim; idem, *Secret Doctrine in Israel,* p. 28; *Holy Kabbalah,* pp. xxvi, 22, 25.

36. Waite, *Doctrine and Literature of the Kabalah,* p. xv. "Eighteen sixty-five" alludes to the apogee of Eliphas Levi (Alphonse Louis Constant), some of whose esoteric works Waite translated; others had been translated by William Wynn Westcott, a founder with Mathers of the Golden Dawn; one of Waite's later efforts was debunking the fraudulent claim (based on forged documents) that Levi had been a member of the Order on the Continent (Howe, *Magicians,* pp. 1–25, especially pp. 17–18).

37. See Stephen on Mrs. Cooper Oakley glimpsing Blavatsky's "elemental" when he is in a context that includes A.E. and Eglinton, those two figures to whom Boyd would devote a chapter of his history of *Ireland's Literary Renaissance* titled "The Dublin Mystics" (*U,* pp. 183–84; see also Stephen's mumblings about "Theosophos" when drunk, p. 409). Compare Ellmann, *James Joyce,* pp. 179–80, on the prank.

38. Madame Blavatsky has often been suggested as a source for Joyce's finger exercises in the esoteric, but it is instructive that although she repeatedly cites Mathers's *Kabbalah Unveiled* (*The Secret Doctrine: The Synthesis of Science, Religion and Philosophy* [1888; 5th Adyan ed., 1962], I, 144; II, 67, 344; III, 294, 313–14; IV, 196; V, 208–11) and on occasion even von Rosenroth's *Kabbalah denudata* (I, 262; II, 106), none of the cited passages that follow in the discussion of Joyce's debts is touched upon in the electic hodge-podge of *The Secret Doctrine.* However, Gershom G. Scholem, *Major Trends in Jewish Mysticism* (1941; reprint ed., New York, 1961), pp. 398–99, has shown her debt to other portions of the *Kabbala denudata* for the "Book Dyzan" upon which Blavatsky's *Secret Doctrine* purports to be a commentary.

39. The kabbalah is "preserved" in the *Sefer Ha-Zohar,* the book of Splendor, which at one time ranked as a canonical text in rabbinic literature. Its eighteen disjunctive sections constitute the commentary of a group of rabbis, allegedly meeting in the second century, who elaborate arabesques around scriptural texts drawn chiefly from Genesis, the Book of Ruth, and the Song of Songs. Purporting to contain and probably reflecting a long oral tradition, the written *Zohar* is the production of Moses ben Shemtob Leon, a wandering Spanish scholar roughly contemporary with Thomas Aquinas. Waite, defending the authenticity of the *Zohar* against multitudinous charges of forgery, calls attention to the differing orders of "literary fabrications" perpetrated by Chatterton, McPherson, and Leon (*Doctrine and Literature of the Kabalah,* pp. 100–103). Of modern studies the most comprehensive background is supplied in Scholem, *Major Trends in Jewish Mysticism.* Presumably without significance is the fact that a text of the Mantuan or "great" Zohar was issued from a Dublin press in 1623. Pico della Mirandola tried to draw the text into the popular syncretism of the early Renaissance in his *Oratione* (*Opere,* ed. Eugenio Garin [Firenze, 1942], I, 155–65); for a context consult Joseph L. Blau, *The Christian Interpretation of the Cabala in the Renaissance* [New York, 1944]; but it was the Baron Knorr von Rosenroth's Latin *Kabbala denudata* that made the work widely accessible.

40. *Holy Kabbalah,* p. 11; see also Waite, *Secret Doctrine in Israel,* pp. 11–12, 257–58, 321, for Waite's original version of this view of kabbalistic reading. If one makes allowance for the bizarre Freudianized abuse of the concept of *zim-zum* (limitation, contraction) as applied to interpretation, there are confirmatory aperçus in Harold Bloom, *Kabbalah and Criticism* (New York, 1975), especially pp. 38–39, 90–91. It is a book that carefully inverts the intention and effect of kabbalistic commentary.

41. We know that, like many initiates of popular mysteries, Joyce both concealed and carefully duplicated and distributed the *Ulysses* schema that was made public in Gilbert's exegesis: see H. K. Croessmann, "Joyce, Gorman and the Schema of *Ulysses:* An Exchange of Letters—Paul L. Leon,

Herbert Gorman, Bennett Cerf," in *James Joyce Miscellany, Second Series* (Carbondale, 1959), pp. 9–14.

42. Waite details how kabbalistic letters combine to denominate "sight," "hearing," "coition," and so on, and also the "directors of man," that is, "the two kidneys, the liver, the gall, the spleen, the colon, the bladder and the arteries" (*Doctrine and Literature of the Kabalah,* pp. 61–63).

43. "We shall come in the end to recognize only one secret doctrine in Jewry, which is the secret concerning sex" (Waite, *Secret Doctrine in Israel,* p. 160; see also p. 227).

44. Ibid., p. 238; see also p. 257.

45. Ibid., p. 247; see also *Zohar,* I, 49b: "It says further of Jacob that 'he tarried there because the sun had set,' which shows that sexual intercourse is forbidden during the day."

46. Waite, *Secret Doctrine in Israel,* p. 238.

47. Ibid., pp. 239, 241; see also *Zohar,* I, 49b–50a.

48. Ellmann, *James Joyce,* p. 278.

49. Mathers, *Kabbalah Unveiled,* p. 49.

50. *Zohar,* I, 56–57a.

51. Waite, *Secret Doctrine in Israel,* p. 108. Gershom G. Scholem, *On the Kabbalah and Its Symbolism* (1960; trans. ed., New York, 1965), pp. 155–57, details the belief that daemonic children (avatars of sin) were begotten by each masturbated seed and came to beleaguer the onanist and his family at the burial. HCE's onanistic guilt is relevant since the Egyptian creation myth of Atem-Ra does not explain it.

52. ". . . according to the Zohar . . . 'there arose not a prophet since in Israel like unto Moses'" (Waite, *Secret Doctrine in Israel,* p. 123). The riddle could have been found, however, in M. Friedlander's translation of Moses Maimonides' *Guide for the Perplexed* (London, 1881), p. xxxii, a text mentioned by Stephen.

53. Waite, *Secret Doctrine in Israel,* p. 198.

54. And even an avatar of Moses: "What selfevident enigma pondered with desultory constancy during 30 years did Bloom now, having effected natural obscurity by the extinction of artificial light, silently suddenly comprehend? Where was Moses when the candle went out?" (*U,* 714).

55. Mathers, *Kabbalah Unveiled,* p. 64. Mathers's laborious efforts are clarified by one clean line of explanation in the *Zohar* (I, 3b) which, however, omits the sexual imagery, important because it invades the plot level of *Ulysses:*

> The Holy and Mysterious One graved in a hidden recess one point. In that He enclosed the whole of Creation as one who locks up all his treasures in a palace, under one key. . . . The palace is provided with fifty mystic gates. They are inserted in its four sides to the number of forty-nine. The one remaining gate is on none of its sides and . . . it is

> hence called the mysterious gate. All these gates have one lock, and there is one tiny spot for the insertion of the key.

Bloom's eastward yearnings are not irrelevant. Ultimately the gates lead, by way of "the Bride of *Macroprosopus,*" to "that place called mystically Zion and Jerusalem" (Waite, *Doctrine and Literature of the Kabalah,* pp. 73–74).

56. "He knows a lot of mixed up things especially about the body and the insides. . . . Poldy anyway whatever he does always wipes his feet on the mat when he comes in . . . and he always takes off his hat when he comes up in the street like that" (*U,* 728, 729).

57. Mathers, *Kabbalah Unveiled,* pp. 26–27. See also p. 34 on the originally androgynous state of all souls, which become separated upon earth into male and female, and Waite, *Doctrine and Literature of the Kabalah,* pp. 227–28.

58. Waite, *Secret Doctrine in Israel,* pp. 193–94.

59. Ibid., pp. 242–44.

60. Ibid., p. 54; Mathers, *Kabbalah Unveiled,* p. 28.

61. *Zohar,* I, 2b–3b, passim; Waite relates the myth in *Secret Doctrine in Israel,* pp. 54–55.

62. I attempted to place this metaphoric action within a complementary context in "The Rhythmic Gesture: Image and Aesthetic in Joyce's *Ulysses,*" *ELH,* 29 (1962), 67–89.

63. *Consubstantial* in this passage is the result of an argument that has made the "son" an aesthetic work produced by the "old father, old artificer."

64. Mathers, *Kabbalah Unveiled,* p. 30; see also pp. 50, 51, 100, 102–3, 104–5, and Waite, *Doctrine and Literature of the Kabalah,* p. 52.

65. Mathers, *Kabbalah Unveiled,* p. 51. The symbolism of the shell is perhaps the most complex to feed into the *Zohar:* see Scholem, *Major Trends in Jewish Mysticism,* pp. 238–39; idem, *On the Kabbalah and Its Symbolism,* pp. 114–17; and Alexander Altmann, "The Motif of the 'Shells' (Qelipoth) in Azriel of Gerona," *Journal of Jewish Studies,* 9 (1958), 73–80. Waite says, "The world of *Assiah,* or of matter, is that into which Adam descended at the Fall, the abode of the evil spirits, the Shells, Envelopes and Cortices of the Kabalah" (*Doctrine and Literature of the Kabalah,* p. 79).

66. Waite, *Secret Doctrine in Israel,* p. 255.

67. Scholem, *Major Trends in Jewish Mysticism,* p. 216.

68. *Holy Kabbalah,* p. 127. See also Waite, *Secret Doctrine in Israel,* pp. 50–51.

69. Mathers, *Kabbalah Unveiled,* pp. 321–22.

70. Ibid., pp. 24–25. See also Waite, *Secret Doctrine in Israel,* pp. 31, 39–40: "Binah is intelligence or understanding . . . and motherhood is its image" (idem, *Doctrine and Literature of the Kabalah,* p. 47).

71. Daniel Mark Fogel examines the positive promise of freedom in the

bowl of saltwater used in the Passover Seder to represent the tears of oppression in Egypt, confirmation of ambivalence in *Binah*'s tears as an aspect of traditional Jewish symbolism ("Symbol and Context in *Ulysses*," pp. 710–14).

72. Mathers, *Kabbalah Unveiled*, p. 307.

73. "In the alternative symbolism. . . . this notion of the Body of God is replaced by that of a Vast Countenance . . . termed the Macroprosopus" (Waite, *Doctrine and Literature of the Kabalah*, pp. 54–55).

74. Mathers, *Kabbalah Unveiled*, p. 144.

75. Ibid., p. 192. See also Waite, *Doctrine and Literature of the Kabalah*, p. 224.

76. Mathers, *Kabbalah Unveiled*, p. 192. Waite levied strictures upon this syncretism, especially as it was manifested in the French translation of the Zohar by de Pauly. See Waite, *Secret Doctrine in Israel*, pp. 202, 215, 224–26, 233–34, 299, 308. But he admits Christian influence upon the resurrectional "doctrines" of the *Zohar* (pp. 188–89).

77. Mathers, *Kabbalah Unveiled*, p. 201.

78. Mathers, *Kabbalah Unveiled*, p. 266. See Mathers, p. 23, on "vibrations"; Waite, *Secret Doctrine in Israel*, p. 194, quoted above; and Cope, "Rhythmic Gesture," pp. 75–76, 87–88.

79. Mathers, *Kabbalah Unveiled*, p. 98. Waite, *Secret Doctrine in Israel*, pp. 191–92, emphasises that the "myrionymous" but principally feminine figure *Shekinah* represents "the waters that are above the firmament in respect of her title of Elohim, but she is the waters below the firmament when she manifests as Adonai."

80. On micturition and micro-macrocosmic fusions in *Ulysses* see Cope, "Rhythmic Gesture," pp. 80–81.

81. St. Augustine, *The City of God*, trans. Marcus Dods (New York, 1950), XI, ii; p. 346.

82. Ibid., XV, iv.

83. Welsh, *City of Dickens*, p. 118.

84. Michael Groden, *"Ulysses" in Progress* (Princeton, 1977), pp. 203–4.

Chapter 5

1. *Marinetti, Selected Writings*, ed. R. W. Flint (New York, 1972), pp. 39–42.

2. Jane Rye, *Futurism* (London, 1972), p. 111; *Le Futurisme* is cited from this source.

3. Marinetti, "The Variety Theater (Sept., 1913)," in *Selected Writings*, pp. 121, 116, respectively. Here, of course, we hear the prelude to Artaud's theater of cruelty.

4. Mason and Ellmann, *Critical Writings*, p. 156. It was a medieval

myth concerning a settlement headed by Scota, a Pharoah's daughter. See James S. Atherton, "Shaun A, Book III, chapter i," in *A Conceptual Guide to "Finnegans Wake,"* ed. Michael H. Begnal and Fritz Senn (University Park, Pa., 1974), pp. 163–64.

5. Did he become aware eventually, commemorating Marinetti as one who "though his heart, soul and spirit turn to pharaoph times, his love, fatih and hope stick to futuerism" (*FW,* 129–30)?

6. Marinetti, *Selected Writings,* p. 164.

7. Edward Bacon, ed., *The Great Archaeologists and Their Discoveries as Originally Reported in the Pages of the "Illustrated London News"* (London, 1976), pp. 173–74.

8. Arthur Power, *Conversations with James Joyce,* ed. Clive Hart (London, 1974), p. 48.

9. Howard Carter and A. C. Mace, *The Tomb of Tutankhamen* (London, 1923), pp. 96–97.

10. William H. Quillan, "Composition of Place: Joyce's Notes on the English Drama," *JJQ,* 13 (1975), 5, 7 (text and facsimile).

11. Frank Budgen, "James Joyce" (*Horizon,* 1941), reprinted in Seon Givens, *James Joyce: Two Decades of Criticism* (1948; reprint ed., New York, 1963), p. 26; see also Budgen, p. 364.

12. Joseph Campbell and Henry Morton Robinson, *A Skeleton Key to "Finnegans Wake"* (New York, 1944), pp. 67, 165, 170, 175, 248; Joseph Campbell, "Finnegan the Wake," in Givens, *Two Decades,* pp. 376–89.

13. James S. Atherton, *The Books at the Wake* (London, 1959), pp. 191–200.

14. Mark L. Troy, *Mummeries of Resurrection: The Cycle of Osiris in "Finnegans Wake"* (Uppsala, 1976). Details dominate this study and continue to be uncovered: see also Troy, "The citye of Is is issuant," *WNL,* 14 (1977), 63; Atherton, "Shaun A, Book III, chapter i" in Begnal and Senn, *Conceptual Guide,* pp. 149–72.

15. Frank Budgen, "The Work in Progress of James Joyce and Old Norse Poetry," *transition,* 13 (summer, 1928), 209–13.

16. Atherton, "Shaun A, Book III, chapter i," in Begnal and Senn, *Conceptual Guide,* p. 157.

17. *Holy Kabbalah,* p. xxxv. Waite's scepticism on relative dating is apparent in *Doctrine and Literature of the Kabalah,* p. 116.

18. Mathers, *Kabbalah Unveiled,* p. 168 n.

19. Harper, *Yeats's Golden Dawn,* pp. 20, 33–35, 62. See also Howe, *Magicians,* pp. 75–103 passim.

20. Howe, *Magicians,* p. 49.

21. Julius Fuerst, *Hebrew and Chaldee Lexicon of the Old Testament* (Leipzig, 1857–61), p. 1, 402.

22. For Moulton's personal and professional history see the sketch by A. S. Peake in *Dictionary of National Biography: Twentieth Century: 1912–*

1921 (Oxford, 1927), and that by W. Fiddian Moulton and A. S. Peake, "James Hope Moulton: 1863–1917," *Bulletin of the John Rylands Library,* 4 (1917), 10–25.

23. James Hope Moulton, *From Egyptian Rubbish-heaps: Five Popular Lectures on the New Testament, with a Sermon,* delivered at Northfield, Massachusetts, in August, 1914 (London, 1st ed., May, 1916; 2nd ed., December, 1917).

24. Ibid., p. 26.

25. Ibid., p. 13.

26. Ibid., pp. 14, 18–19.

27. See also another version of "om omominous letters and widely signed pieces of pottery" (*FW,* 543).

28. Moulton, *Egyptian Rubbish-heaps,* p. 16.

29. In arguing the antiquity of the formulae from the *Book of the Dead,* Budge had cited their appearance on the broken sarcophagus of the Fourth Dynasty ruler Men-kau-Ra (Mycerinus), quoting Raven's account of its discovery "at the bottom of the rubbish" (E. A. Wallis Budge, *The Book of the Dead: The Papyrus of Ani in the British Museum* [London, 1895], p. xx). This edition was that presumably owned by Crosby and used by Joyce; in any case, it is cited in *Finnegans Wake,* as pointed out by Atherton (*Books at the Wake,* pp. 192–93.).

30. Moulton, *Egyptian Rubbish-heaps,* p. 15.

31. Campbell and Robinson, *Skeleton Key,* pp. 103–5; and Atherton, *Books at the Wake,* pp. 61–66.

32. Moulton, *Egyptian Rubbish-heaps,* p. 13.

33. Ibid., p. 14.

34. Mumford, *The City in History,* pp. 6–10 passim.

35. Ibid., pp. 81–82.

36. E. A. Wallis Budge, *The Book of the Dead: An English Translation* (London, 1923), II, 290.

37. Mark Schechner, *Joyce in Nighttown* (Berkeley, 1974), p. 49.

38. E. A. Wallis Budge, *The Egyptian Religion of Resurrection: Osiris* (1912; reprint ed., New York, 1961), II, 203.

39. Ibid., II, 330.

40. Henri Frankfort, *Kingship and the Gods* (Chicago, 1948), p. 28.

41. Robert Thomas Rundle Clark, *Myth and Symbol in Ancient Egypt* (New York, 1960), pp. 40 ff.

42. For a selection see pp. 4–6, 37, 40, 56, 63–66, 97, 108, 111, 160, 182–85, 194, 223–24, 261, 278–79, 317–18, 338, 342–44, 435, 467, 499, which represent only masturbatory passages embedded in a clearly Egyptian context.

43. Budge, *Osiris,* I, 328.

44. Ibid., I, 328.

INDEX

The note number is given when a note contains a substantive discussion of the topic.

The Johns Hopkins University Press

This book was set in IBM Aldine Roman text by Horne Associates, Inc., and AM International Trump Medieval display type by Alpha Graphics, Inc., from a design by Alan Carter. It was printed on 50-lb. No. 66 Eggshell Cream Offset and bound by Universal Lithographers.